Rufus Wheelwright Clark

The African slave trade

Rufus Wheelwright Clark

The African slave trade

ISBN/EAN: 9783744737357

Printed in Europe, USA, Canada, Australia, Japan

Cover: Foto ©ninafisch / pixelio.de

More available books at **www.hansebooks.com**

THE

AFRICAN SLAVE TRADE.

BY

REV. RUFUS W. CLARK.

PUBLISHED BY THE
AMERICAN TRACT SOCIETY,
28 CORNHILL, BOSTON.

CONTEI

CHAPTER V.

FAILURE OF MEASURES TO DESTROY THE SLAVE TRADE.

CHAPTER VI.

EVIDENCES OF THE REVIVAL OF THE SLAVE TRADE IN THE UNITED STATES.

CHAPTER VII.

CONCLUSION.

THE AFRICAN SLAVE TRADE.

CHAPTER I.

THE QUESTION AT ISSUE.

Ecclesiastes iv. 1. So I returned, and considered all the oppressions that are done under the sun: and behold the tears of *such as were* oppressed, and they had no comforter; and on the side of their oppressors *there was* power; but they had no comforter.

It is certainly surprising, that in this nineteenth century, and under the light of free and Christian institutions, we should be called upon to discuss anew the subject of the African slave trade. It was supposed that the inexpediency and iniquity of this traffic were universally conceded ; that the efforts of philanthropic and Christian men, upon two continents, to enlighten public opinion, had been successful ; and that the action of our government and the governments of Europe, in abolishing said traffic, was regarded as final.

But for several years past there has been growing up in the community a power that plants itself in direct antagonism to the teachings of our religion, the professed aim of our political institutions, the influence of our educational systems, and the sentiments inculcated in our national literature. A battle is in progress between liberty and slavery, God's truth and the vile passions of men, that perils the existence of this republic, and touches every vital interest. And, to crown the triumphs of the slave power, we again have vessels fitting out in our ports, north and south, to bring to our shores the suffering children of Africa, and entail anew upon that continent and our own, the evils and horrors of this accursed traffic.

It may be a delicate question to inquire who, in the various States of this Union, are responsible for the growth of this evil; who, by their direct action, their silence, or their apologies for slavery, have made contributions to its strength. To his own conscience, and before God, each man must answer.

When benevolent societies, ecclesiastical bodies, an influential press, churches professing to be Christian, unite with a demoralized public opinion, and an oppressive secular authority, to perpetuate or extend a system of iniquity, there is created a force for evil, against which even millions of free Christian men find it difficult to contend. The virus enters the arteries and muscles of the national life, palsies the sinews of the natural strength, and poisons the fountains of national existence. And who will answer for the consequences of fostering such an evil in the heart of a country blessed as ours has been by Heaven? Have we received any special license to sin, with an exemption from the action of those eternal laws that bind the penalty to the transgression?

Is it not true now, as of the past, that " the nation and kingdom that will not serve Thee shall perish, yea, those nations shall be utterly wasted "? Could the spirits of departed American heroes return, with what increased emphasis would they reiterate the burning words that expressed their feelings and principles on this momentous question!

Referring to the struggle for American independence, and the palpable inconsistency of those who achieved it, Thomas Jefferson said:

"What an incomprehensible machine is man, who can endure toil, famine, stripes, imprisonment, and death itself, in vindication of his own liberty, and the next moment be deaf to all those motives whose power supported him through his trial, and inflict on his fellow-men a bondage, one hour of which is fraught with more misery than ages of that which he rose in rebellion to oppose! . . Can the liberties of a nation be thought secure, when we have removed their only firm basis, a conviction in the minds of the people that these liberties are the gift of God? That they are not to be violated but with his wrath? *Indeed, I tremble for my country, when I reflect that God is just;* that his justice can not sleep for ever; that, considering numbers, nature, and natural means only, a revolution of the wheel of fortune, an exchange of situation, is among possible events; that it may become probable by supernatural interference. *The Almighty has no attribute which can take side with us in such a contest.*"

If, then, every attribute of the Almighty is against the continuance of this system of oppression, with what feelings must he view the efforts to revive the traffic in human beings, in the face of the existing light and wide-spread knowledge of the evils of slavery! We tremble when we remember that God is just, and that *his justice can not sleep for ever.*

It is true that there are persons, not a few, who do not recognize the views and attributes of the Almighty, when considering this question. The idea of a higher power than that of the slave power, has been, over and over again, treated with a sneer of contempt, in circles where we had a right to look for better things. Language has been used, and principles have been set forth, by professed teachers of public morals, that tend to sap the foundations of all morality, blunt the public conscience, bring contempt upon the religion of the Bible, and provoke the wrath of Heaven. And unless the nation will learn, by the teachings of revelation, and the ordinary course of divine providence, that there is a government above all human governments, and a power to which human authorities are amenable, we shall learn it in another way, and perhaps by a bitter experience. The words of Patrick Henry, the apostle of liberty, which he uttered in 1773, are peculiarly applicable to the present day. He said:

"It is not a little surprising, that the professors of Christianity, whose chief excellence consists in softening the human heart, in cherishing and improving its finer feelings, should encourage a practice so totally repugnant to the first impressions of right and wrong. What adds to the wonder is, that this abominable practice has been introduced in the most enlightened ages. Times that seem to have pretensions to boast of high improvements in the arts and sciences, and refined morality, have brought into general use, and guarded by many laws, a species of violence and tyranny, which our more rude and barbarous, but more honest ancestors detested. Is it not amazing, that at a time when the rights of humanity are defined and understood with precision, in a country, above all others, fond of liberty,— that in such an age, and in such a country, we find men professing a religion the most humane, mild, gentle, and generous, yet adopting a principle as repugnant to humanity as it is inconsistent with the Bible, and destructive to liberty ? Every thinking, honest man rejects it in speculation. How few in practice, from conscientious motives ! "

Indeed, to express our views of slavery and the slave trade, we could not employ more intense and truthful words than were uttered by the men who participated in the struggle for American liberty, who were members of the convention that framed the Constitution of the United States, and the leaders of public opinion in the early history of our nation.

We might quote the language of Gouverneur Morris, of Pennsylvania, who, early in the convention, said, " He never would concur in upholding domestic slavery. It was a nefarious institution. It was the curse of Heaven ! "

The general opinion existing at that time is expressed by John Jay, James Monroe, James Madison, Benjamin Franklin, and the immortal Washington. Mr. Jay was known as the earnest and uncompromising advocate of freedom. In one of his letters from Spain, he wrote as follows:

" The State of New York is rarely out of my mind or heart, and I am often disposed to write much respecting its affairs; but I have so little information as to its present political objects and operations, that I am afraid to attempt it. An excellent law might be made out of the Pennsylvania one, for the gradual abolition of slavery. Till America comes into this measure, her prayers to Heaven will be impious. This is a strong expression, but it is just. Were I in your legislature, I would present a bill for the purpose with great care, and I would never cease moving it till it became a law, or I ceased to be a member. I believe that God governs the world, and I believe it to be a maxim in his, as in our court, that those who ask for equity ought to do it."

Can any principles be clearer, more just, more humane than these?

The opinions and feelings of Washington, who was President of the Convention that formed the Constitution, may be gathered from his letters. In one addressed to Robert Morris, Esq., he said:

" I hope that it will not be conceived from these observations, that it is my wish to hold the unhappy people who are the subject of this letter, in slavery. I can only say, that there is not a man living, who wishes more sincerely than I do, to see a plan adopted for the abolition of it; but there is only one proper and effectual mode by which it can be accomplished, and that is, by the legislative authority; *and this, as far as my suffrage will go, shall not be wanting.*"

In another to John F. Mercer, Esq., he said :

"I never mean, unless some particular circumstance should compel me to it, to possess another slave by purchase ; *it being among my first wishes to see some plan adopted by which slavery in this country may be abolished by law.*"

In writing to Gen. Lafayette, he said :

" The benevolence of your heart, my dear Marquis, is so conspicuous on all occasions, that I never wonder at fresh proofs of it; but your late purchase of an estate in the colony of Cayenne, with a view of emancipating the slaves, is a generous and noble proof of your humanity. Would to God, a like spirit might diffuse itself generally into the minds of the people in this country."

These opinions, and many others that we might adduce, bearing against slavery as it existed at that period, bear, with augmented power, against the foreign traffic in slaves. Indeed, it was the influence of these very opinions, and the persevering efforts of these heroes, that secured the passage of the law for the abolition of the slave trade.

Having just emerged from the contest to secure American liberty, the inconsistency of upholding the slave traffic was too glaring not to be seen by every honest mind. And, at that time, under the tuition of the great American struggle, the hostility to slavery was national, and the pro-slavery spirit was local, and mainly confined to those having a pecuniary interest in slaves. The system was looked upon as a temporary domestic evil, rather than as a permanent institution, and the Constitution was framed with reference to its gradual and final extinction.

Indeed, the political philosophy that underlay the American revolution, embraced not simply the freedom of this nation, but the rights of human nature. This was the animating spirit of the movement, as directly opposed to the evil we are considering as light is opposed to darkness.

Alexander Hamilton directed against the odious stamp act the authority of British law, as he found it written down by Blackstone.

" The law of nature, being coëval with God himself, is, of course, superior to any other. It is binding over all the globe, in all countries, and at all times. No human laws are of any validity if contrary to this, and such of them as are valid derive all their authority, mediately or immediately, from this original."

Then, as if disdaining to stand on any mere human authority, however high, the framer of the American Constitution declared :

" The sacred rights of mankind are not to be rummaged for among old parchments or musty records. They are written, as with a sunbeam, in the whole volume of human nature, and can never be erased or obscured by mortal power."

Lafayette closed his review of the Revolution, when returning to France, with this beautiful and glowing apostrophe :

"May this great temple which we have just erected to liberty, always be an instruction to oppressors, an example to the oppressed, a refuge for the rights of the human race, and an object of delight to the manes of its founders."

"Happy," (said Washington, when announcing the treaty of peace to the army,) "thrice happy shall they be pronounced hereafter, who shall have contributed any thing, who shall have performed the meanest office in erecting this stupendous fabric of freedom and empire on the broad basis of independency, who shall have assisted in protecting the rights of human nature, and establishing an asylum for the poor and oppressed of all nations and religions."

And would that the solemn injunction uttered at the close of the Convention that adopted the Federal Constitution might be sounded, in trumpet peals, through the length and breadth of our land. Said those noble patriots, *"Let it be remembered, that it has ever been the pride and boast of America, that the rights for which she contended were* THE RIGHTS OF HUMAN NATURE." How far the present generation has fallen from that sublime principle, I need not stop to show. That a fearful responsibility rests somewhere upon the creators of public opinion, in state and church, at this day, I solemnly believe.

One cause of this rapid retrograde movement is, doubtless, the strong effort that has been made to separate the evil of the extension of slavery and the revival of the trade, from the evil of the system itself.

Many have taken the ground, that while they were opposed to the introduction of slavery into new territories, and to the revival of the traffic, they would not interfere with it where it was an established institution. But the arguments employed against its extension or increase, if they have any force, lie equally against the system in any locality. If it is an evil in Kansas, it is just as much an evil in Virginia. If it is wrong to capture the African on his own soil, and subject him to the horrors of the slave ship, then it is wrong to retain him in slavery. And wherever an evil exists on the face of the earth, it is the duty of every honest man to express his convictions concerning it, and to do what lies legitimately in his power to remove it.

Much sophistry has been advanced on this point to strengthen the slave power, which has corrupted the public opinion in regard to our individual responsibility in relation to the evil.

In the early history of the country, our statesmen and theologians regarded slavery and the slave trade as one in nature and sinfulness.

In 1794, the General Assembly of the Presbyterian Church of the United States expressed its opinion in the following language :

"1 Tim. i. 10. The law is made for man-stealers. This crime, among the Jews, exposed the perpetrators of it to capital punishment; Exodus xxi. 16; and the apostle here classes them with sinners of the first rank. The word he uses, in its original import, comprehends all who are concerned in bringing any of the human race into slavery, or in retaining them in it. *Hominum fures, qui servos vel liberos abducunt, retinent, vendunt, vel emunt.* Stealers of men are all those who bring off slaves or free men, and keep, sell, or buy them. To steal a free man, says Grotius, is the highest kind of theft. In other instances, we only steal human property; but when we steal or retain men in slavery, we seize those who, in common with ourselves, are constituted, by the original grant, lords of the earth. Genesis i. 28. *Vide* Poli synopsin in loc."

The state of public feeling in the year 1818, is indicated in the views expressed at that period by the same body, as may be seen in " The Digest of the General Assembly," from which the following extract is made :

" The General Assembly of the Presbyterian Church, having taken into consideration the subject of slavery, think proper to make known their sentiments upon it.

" We consider the voluntary enslaving of one part of the human race by another, as a gross violation of the most precious and sacred rights of human nature ; as utterly inconsistent with the law of God, which requires us to love our neighbor as ourselves; and as totally irreconcilable with the spirit and principles of the gospel of Christ, which enjoins that ' all things whatsoever ye would that men should do to you, do ye even so to them.' Slavery creates a paradox in the moral system; it exhibits rational, accountable, and immortal beings in such circumstances as scarcely to leave them the power of moral action. It exhibits them as dependent on the will of others, whether they shall receive religious instruction ; whether they shall know and worship the true God; whether they shall enjoy the ordinances of the gospel; whether they shall perform the duties, and cherish the endearments of husbands and wives, parents and chil-

2

dren, neighbors and friends; whether they shall preserve their chastity and purity, or regard the dictates of justice and humanity. Such are some of the consequences of slavery; consequences not imaginary, but which connect themselves with its very existence. The evils to which the slave is always exposed, often take place in their very worst degree and form; and where all of them do not take place, still the slave is deprived of his natural rights, degraded as a human being, and exposed to the danger of passing into the hands of a master, who may inflict upon him all the hardships and injuries which inhumanity and avarice may suggest.

"It is manifestly the duty of all Christians, when the inconsistency of slavery with the dictates of humanity and religion has been demonstrated, and is generally seen and acknowledged, to use their honest, earnest, and unwearied endeavors, as speedily as possible, to efface this blot on our holy religion, and *to obtain the complete abolition of slavery throughout the world.*"

This is the precise language that that learned and pious body of men, at that time used. They desired, and they looked forward to, "the complete abolition of slavery throughout the world."

The slave trade they regarded as abolished, so far as the verdict of Christian nations could secure this end. And they were not troubled with any mawkish sensibility about expressing their views of the evils of the system, as they saw them under their own eye. The idea of throttling the slave trade with one hand, and feeding domestic slavery with the other, was one that never occurred to them. This is a modern invention, for which the present generation must have all the credit.

CHAPTER II.

HISTORY OF THE SLAVE TRADE.

Exodus xxi. 16. And he that stealeth a man, and selleth him, or if he be found in his hand, he shall surely be put to death.

> See the dire victim torn from social life,
> The shrieking babe, the agonizing wife!
> She, wretch forlorn, is dragged by hostile hands,
> To distant tyrants, sold to distant lands,
> Transmitted miseries and successive chains,
> The sole sad heritage her child obtains!
> E'en this last wretched boon their foes deny,
> To live together, or together die.
> By felon hands, by one relentless stroke,
> See the fond links of feeling nature broke!
> The fibers twisting round a parent's heart,
> Torn from their grasp, and bleeding as they part.
> What wrongs, what injuries does Oppression plead,
> To smooth the crime and sanctify the deed?
> What strange offense, what aggravated sin?
> They stand convicted — of a darker skin!
>
> HANNAH MORE.

THE commencement of this nefarious traffic dates back to the year 1503, when a few slaves were sent from the Portuguese settlements in Africa to the Spanish colonies in America. It is said, however, that before that period, in 1434, a Portuguese captain landed in Guinea, and captured some colored lads, whom he sold at a profit to the Moors settled in the south of Spain. The trade became established in Spain in the year 1517, when Charles V.

granted to Lebresa the exclusive right to import annually 4000 Africans, who were sold to the Genoese. The French under Louis XIII., and the English in the reign of Queen Elizabeth, permitted the traffic, under the plea that the captives taken in war would thus be saved from death; although Elizabeth protested against the cruelties connected with the trade.

The African chiefs, stimulated by a desire for gain, waged war against their neighbors, and thousands were soon captured, and hurried to the coast, to be exchanged for rum, brandy, iron, and toys, which constituted the currency of Europeans in this traffic. The most unjust and cruel means were resorted to in order to carry on the inhuman barter. Peaceful villages were ruthlessly invaded; the innocent were charged with crimes that they never committed; children were torn from their parents, and bound together, two and two, by the neck, with heavy pieces of wood, and marched, or rather driven to the river or coast, where a multitude of purchasers were ready to place them on board their vessels, and doom them to all the horrors of the *middle passage.* Thus this traffic was conceived in sin, and baptized in every form of iniquity.*

* For more extended evidences than our limits will allow us to present, see "The Slave Trade and Remedy," by Sir T. F. Buxton; Clarkson's "History of the Abolition of the Slave Trade;" Mr R. Walsh's "Notices of Brazil;" "Articles in Edinburgh Encyclopædia," and "Encyclopædia Americana;" "Benezet's Account of Africa;" "Dupries's Residence in Ashantee," London, 1824. "Life of Ashmun."

In the year 1620, the same year in which the Pilgrims landed on Plymouth Rock, bringing with them liberty, virtue, and a pure faith, a Dutch vessel landed twenty negroes at Queenstown, Virginia, who were sold to the colonists as slaves, thus opening the trade with our country. The traffic thus sustained by Portugal, Spain, France, and England, and having a new field on this continent, gradually advanced, producing every where its legitimate and terrible effects. So anxious were the petty African kings to keep up the trade, that when the French revolution lessened the demand for human merchandise, the king of Dahomey sent, in 1796, his brother and son to Lisbon, to secure the revival of the traffic, and entered into a treaty in favor of Portugal.

Before this traffic was opened, and the Africans were corrupted by drunkenness and avarice, wars seldom occurred; but the introduction of this wickedness opened the door to every crime, and it has frequently happened that thousands have been slain, while only hundreds have been captured. A surgeon, who sailed from New York to engage in the slave trade, made the following record in his journal: "The commander of the vessel sent to acquaint the king that he wanted a cargo of slaves. Some time after, the king sent him word he had not yet met with the desired success. A battle was fought, which lasted three days. Four thousand five hundred men were slain upon the spot!"

Some idea of the waste of life which this iniquity

has occasioned may be gained, when we remember that during the last three centuries about forty millions of human beings have been torn from Africa, for the purpose of being reduced to servitude. Besides the loss in war, from fifteen to twenty per cent. die on the passage, and many more die after being landed.*

The gifted and humane Wilberforce, in a speech before Parliament,† remarked that:

" He would now say a few words relative to the " middle passage," principally to show that regulations could not effect a cure of the evil there. Mr. Isaac Wilson had stated in his evidence, that the ship in which he sailed, only three years ago, was of three hundred and seventy tons, and that she carried six hundred and two slaves. Of these she lost one hundred and fifty-five. There were three or four other vessels in company with her, which belonged to the same

* Fifty years ago the Christian (!) slave trade was 80,000 annually ; now 200,000 ! Mohammedan slave trade, 50,000 annually. The aggregate loss of life in the Christian trade, in the successive stages of seizure, march, detention, middle passage, after landing, and seasoning, is 145 per cent., or 1,450 for every 1,000 available for use in the end ; and 100 per cent. loss of life, by the same causes, in the Mohammedan trade. Consequently, the annual victims of the Christian slave trade are 375,600 ; of the Mohammedan, 100,000. Total loss to Africa, 475,000 annually ; or, 23,750,000 in half a century, at the same rate.

A slave ship named JEHOVAH (!) made three voyages between Brazil and Angola in thirteen months, of 1836-7, and landed 700 slaves the first voyage, 600 the second, and 520 the third, — in all, 1820. — Buxton.

The single town of Liverpool, England, realized in this traffic, before its abolition in that empire, a net profit of more than $100,-000,000 ! — History of Liverpool.

† From Clarkson's " History of the Abolition of the Slave Trade."

owners. One of these carried four hundred and fifty, and buried two hundred; another carried four hundred and sixty-six, and buried seventy-three; another five hundred and forty-six, and buried one hundred and fifty-eight; and from the four together, after the landing of their cargoes, two hundred and twenty died. He fell in with another vessel, which had lost three hundred and sixty-two, but the number which had been bought was not specified. Now if to these actual deaths, during and immediately after the voyage, we were to add the subsequent loss in the seasoning, and to consider that this would be greater than ordinary in cargoes which were landed in such a sickly state, we should find a mortality, which, if it were only general for a few months, would entirely depopulate the globe.

"He would advert to what Mr. Wilson said, when examined, as a surgeon, as to the causes of these losses, and particularly on board his own ship, where he had the means of ascertaining them. The substance of his reply was this:— that most of the slaves labored under a fixed melancholy, which now and then broke out into lamentations and plaintive songs, expressive of the loss of their relations, friends, and country. So powerful did this sorrow operate, that many of them attempted in various ways to destroy themselves, and three actually effected it. Others obstinately refused to take sustenance; and when the whip, and other violent means, were used to compel them to eat, they looked up into the face of the officer, who unwillingly executed this painful task, and said, with a smile, in their own language, ' Presently we shall be no more.' This, their unhappy state of mind, produced a general languor and debility, which were increased in many instances by an unconquerable aversion to food, arising partly from sickness, and partly, to use the language of slave captains, from sulkiness. These causes naturally produced the flux. The contagion spread; several were carried off daily; and the disorder, aided by so many powerful auxiliaries, resisted the power of medicine. And it was worth while to remark, that these grievous sufferings were not owing either to want of care on the part of the owners, or to any negligence or harshness of the captain; for Mr. Wilson declared, that his ship was as well fitted out, and the crew and slaves as well treated, as any body could reasonably expect."

After giving other testimony, Mr. Wilberforce added:

" Such were the evils of the passage. But evils were conspicuous every where in this trade. Never was there, indeed, a system so replete with wickedness and cruelty. To whatever part of it we turned our eyes, whether to Africa, the middle passage, or the West Indies, we could find no comfort, no satisfaction, no relief. It was the gracious ordinance of Providence, both in the natural and moral world, that good should often arise out of evil. Hurricanes cleared the air; and the propagation of truth was promoted by persecution. Pride, vanity, and profusion contributed often, in their remoter consequences, to the happiness of mankind. In common, what was itself evil and vicious was permitted to carry along with it some circumstances of palliation. The Arab was hospitable; the robber brave. We did not necessarily find cruelty associated with fraud, or meanness with injustice. But here the case was far otherwise. It was the prerogative of this detestable traffic to separate from evil its concomitant good, and to reconcile discordant mischiefs. It robbed war of its generosity; it deprived peace of its security; we saw in it the vices of polished society, without its knowledge or its comforts; and the evils of barbarism, without its simplicity. No age, no sex, no rank, no condition, was exempt from the fatal influence of this wide-wasting calamity. Thus it attained to the fullest measure of pure, unmixed, unsophisticated wickedness; and, scorning all competition and comparison, it stood without a rival in the secure, undisputed possession of its detestable preëminence."

The discussion in the British Parliament, while the question of the abolition of the slave trade was pending, brought out from the noble champions of freedom an array of facts that ought to arouse all Christian nations to the barbarities of this traffic. But the Christian nations need to be Christianized, especially this American nation, that is madly plunging anew into this accursed traffic. We need in an American congress a William Wilberforce, a Charles James Fox, a William Pitt, an Edmund Burke, a Thomas Erskine, a Granville Sharp, and a Thomas Clarkson, to move the nation, as these noble men moved the British public, and thunder into the ears of the people the crimes and cruelties of man-stealing, until they rise in their might, and decree its annihilation.

It is impossible to conceive a more foul blot upon the American name, than the revival of this traffic at a day like this. It is reversing the wheels of civilization, and voluntarily going back to barbarism. It is giving the lie to our boasts of intelligence, humanity, and freedom. It is directly bidding defiance to the Almighty, and calling down the wrath of Heaven. It is adding a chapter to the history of this trade, the darkest, the most fearful and terrible that was ever written. "Enlightened age!" "Christian nation!" "Free America!" Let us not mock the common sense of the world by the use of these phrases, while this dark cloud is casting its shadow over us. Let us, at least, pray for deliverance from the lowest form of national hypocrisy.

We would gladly omit the details of the sufferings incident to what is called the middle passage, but we can not do justice, even to a brief survey of the traffic, without adding one or two of the many testimonies on this point. And while gazing upon a single picture, if we will multiply these by thousands, we may approximate towards a realization of a passage across the Atlantic in a slaver, and be prompted to do what lies in our power to drive this master iniquity from the face of the earth.

In a debate on the slave trade. Mr. Fox justly remarked that:

"True humanity consists not in a squeamish ear; it consists not in starting, and shrinking at such tales as these, but in a disposition of heart to relieve misery. True humanity appertains rather to the mind than the nerves, and prompts men to use real and active endeavors to execute the actions which it suggests."

Would that the emotions excited by narratives like the following, might lead to the formation of principles, the expression of opinions, and the adoption of vigorous measures, that would roll back the tide of this gigantic sin. Mr. Walsh, in his "Notices of Brazil," published in London in 1830, and in Boston in 1832, thus describes a slave ship examined by the English man-of-war in which he returned from Brazil, in May, 1829 :

" She had taken in, on the coast of Africa, three hundred and thirty-six males, and two hundred and twenty-six females, making in all five hundred and sixty-two, and had been out seventeen days. The slaves were all enclosed under grated hatchways, between decks. The space was so low that they sat between each other's legs, and were stowed so close together that there was no possibility of their lying down, or at all changing their position, by night or day. As they belonged to, and were shipped on account of different individuals, they were all branded, like sheep, with the owners' marks, of different forms. These were impressed under their breasts, or on their arms, and, as the mate informed me, with perfect indifference, ' Queimados pelo ferro quento, — burnt with red-hot iron.' Over the hatchway stood a ferocious looking fellow, with a scourge of many twisted thongs in his hand, who was the slave-driver of the ship; and whenever he heard the slightest noise below, he shook it over them, and seemed eager to exercise it. As soon as the poor creatures saw us looking down at them, their dark and melancholy visages brightened up.

" They perceived something of sympathy and kindness in our looks, which they had not been accustomed to, and feeling, instinctively, that we were friends, they immediately began to shout and clap their hands. One or two had picked up a few Portuguese words, and cried out, ' Viva!

viva!' The women were particularly excited They all held up their arms, and when we bent down and shook hands with them, they could not contain their delight; they endeavored to scramble upon their knees, stretching up to kiss our hands, and we understood that they knew we had come to liberate them. Some, however, hung down their heads, in apparently hopeless dejection; some were greatly emaciated, and some, particularly children, seemed dying. But the circumstance which struck us most forcibly, was how it was possible for such a number of human beings to exist, packed up and wedged together as tight as they could cram, in low cells, three feet high, the greater part of which, except that immediately under the grated hatchway, was shut out from light, or air, and this when the thermometer, exposed to the open sky, was standing, in the shade on our deck, at 89°. The space between decks was divided into two compartments, three feet three inches high; the size of one was sixteen feet by eighteen, and of the other forty by twenty-one; into the first were crammed the women and girls; into the second the men and boys. Two hundred and twenty-six fellow creatures were thus thrust into one space two hundred and eighty-eight feet square, and three hundred and thirty-six into another space eight hundred feet square, giving to the whole an average of twenty-three inches, and to each of the women not more than thirteen inches, though many of them were pregnant. We also found manacles, and fetters of different kinds; but it appears that they had all been taken off before we boarded. The heat of these horrid places was so great, and the odor so offensive, that it was quite impossible to enter there, even had there been room. They were measured, as above, when the slaves left them. The officers insisted that the poor suffering creatures should be admitted on deck, to get air and water. This was opposed by the mate of the slaver, who, from a feeling that they deserved it, declared that they would murder them all. The officers, however, persisted, and the poor beings were all turned up together. It is impossible to conceive the effect of this eruption; five hundred and seven fellow creatures, of all ages and sexes, some children, some adults, some old men and women, all in a state of total nudity, scrambling out together to taste the luxury of a little fresh air and water.

" They came swarming up, like bees from the aperture of a hive, till the whole deck was crowded to suffocation, from stem to stern; so that it was impossible to imagine where they could all have come from, or how they could all have been stowed away. On looking into the places where they had been crammed, there were found some children, next to the side of the ship, in the places most remote from light and air; they were lying nearly in a torpid state, after the rest had turned out. The little creatures seemed indifferent as to life or death, and when they were carried on deck, many of them could not stand.

"After enjoying for a short time the unusual luxury of air, some water was brought; it was then that the extent of their sufferings was exposed in a fearful manner. They all rushed like maniacs towards it. No entreaties, or threats, or blows could restrain them; they shrieked, and struggled, and fought with one another for a drop of this precious liquid, as if they grew rabid at the sight of it. There is nothing from which slaves, in the mid-passage, suffer so much, as want of water. It is sometimes usual to take out casks filled with sea-water as ballast, and when the slaves are received on board, to start the casks, and refill them with fresh. On one occasion, a ship from Bahia neglected to change the contents of the casks, and on the mid-passage found, to their horror, that they were filled with nothing but salt water. All the slaves on board perished! We could judge of the extent of their sufferings from the afflicting sight we now saw.

" When the poor creatures were ordered down again, several of them came and pressed their heads against our knees, with looks of the greatest anguish, at the prospect of returning to the horrid place of suffering below."

The devoted philanthropist, Granville Sharp, presented a case to the British public that justly aroused their indignation. It shows the power of avarice to obliterate the last vestiges of humanity, and convert men into devils.

" From the trial, it appeared that the ship Zong, Luke Collingwood master, sailed from the island of St. Thomas, on the coast of Africa, September 6, 1781, with four hundred and forty slaves, and fourteen whites on board, for Jamaica, and that in the November following she fell in with that island; but, instead of proceeding to some port, the master, mistaking, as he alleges, Jamaica for Hispaniola, ran her to leeward. Sickness and mortality had by this time taken place on board the crowded vessel; so that, between the time of leaving the coast of Africa and the 29th of November, sixty slaves and seven white people had died, and a great number of the surviving slaves were then sick, and not likely to live.

" On that day, the master of the ship called together a few of the officers, and stated to them, that if the sick slaves died a natural death, the loss would fall on the owners of the ship, — it would be the loss of the underwriters; alleging, at the same time, that it would be less cruel to throw the sick wretches into the sea, than to suffer them to linger out a few days under the disorder with which they were afflicted.

" To this inhuman proposal the mate, James Kelsal, at first objected; but Collingwood at length prevailed on the crew to listen to it. He then chose out from the cargo one hundred and thirty-two slaves, and brought them on deck, all, or most of whom were sickly, and not likely to recover, and he ordered the crew by turns to throw them into the sea. 'A parcel' of them were accordingly thrown overboard, and, on counting over the remainder, next morning, it appeared that the number so drowned had been fifty-four. He then ordered another parcel to be thrown over, which, on a second counting, on the succeeding day, was proved to have amounted to forty-two.

" On the third day, the remaining thirty-six were brought on deck, and, as these now resisted the cruel purpose of their masters, the arms of twenty-six were fettered with irons, and the savage crew proceeded with the diabolical work, casting them down to join their comrades of the former days. Outraged misery could endure no longer; the ten last victims sprang disdainfully from the grasp of their tyrants, defied their power, and, leaping into the sea, felt a momentary triumph in the embrace of death."

These statements, distressing as they are, only afford us a specimen of the barbarities and horrors of this crime. The cruelties of the African slave trade have never been written, — can not be written. No pen can describe them; and yet, how many American citizens, whose feelings will revolt at these details of suffering, will hear with comparative indifference of the revival of the iniquity in our land !

CHAPTER III.

Isaiah xlii. 22. But this is a people robbed and spoiled; *they are* all of them snared in holes, and they are hid in prison houses ; they are for a prey, and none delivereth, for a spoil, and none saith, Restore.

In forming an estimate of the evils of the slave trade, its disastrous influence upon Africa itself has not been, in this country, duly considered.

While it has been the duty of Christian nations to give to the benighted inhabitants on that continent the gospel, and its blessed, civil, social, and domestic institutions, they have, instead, entailed upon them a series of the worst evils and calamities that can afflict mankind.

Besides the sufferings, and fearful waste of human life, to which we have referred, the slave trade has stood for centuries as a barrier to the moral and social improvement of the people. It has shut out the light of knowledge, the refining and elevating influences of civilization, and the precious truths and glorious hopes of Christianity. It has paralyzed industry, discouraged agriculture, prevented the establishment of commercial relations

with other nations, rendered property and life inse-
cure, kindled the spirit of war, and fostered the
vilest passions. It has plunged millions of our
fellow-men into the lowest depths of superstition
and barbarism. It has added blackness to the darkness of heathenism, rent asunder natural ties, rendered savage life more savage, and perpetuated the
reign of anguish and despair. Justly did John
Wesley, in a moment of burning indignation, desig-
nate this trade as "the execrable sum of all vil-
lanies."

We have no means of accurately describing the
condition of Africa previous to the traffic in slaves,
as so little intercourse had existed between that
country and the nations of Europe. But Sir T. F.
Buxton has collected, in his work on the "Slave
Trade and its Remedy," proofs that the people were
in a more prosperous condition at that time than
they have been since the commerce in slaves was
opened. He says: "It is remarkable that the
geographers, Nubiensis in the 12th century, and
Leo Africanus in the 16th, state that in their time
the people between the Senegal and Gambia
never made war on each other, but employed themselves in keeping their herds, and in tilling the
ground. When Sir I. Hawkins visited Africa, in
1562–7, with intent to seize the people, he found the
land well cultivated, bearing plenty of grain and
fruit, and the towns prettily laid out." *

* ARCHBISHOP SHARP, the grandfather of Granville Sharp, in a ser-

3

"Bozman, about 1700, writes that it was the early European settlers who first sowed dissensions among the natives of Africa, for the sake of purchasing their prisoners of war. Benezet quotes William Smith who was sent by the African Company in 1726, to visit their settlement, and who stated, from the testimony of a factor who had lived ten years in the country, that the discerning natives accounted it their greatest unhappiness ever to have been visited by Europeans."

Dupries, in a journey to Coomassie, in 1819, thus describes the country then recently laid waste by the king of Ashantee: * "From the Praa, southward, the progress of the sword down to the margin of the sea, may be traced by moldering ruins, desolate plantations, and osseous relics; such are the traits of negro ferocity. The inhabitants, whether Assins or Fantees, whose youth and beauty exempted them from slaughter on the spot, were only reserved to grace a triumph in the metropolis of their conquerors, where they were again subject to a scru-

mon preached before the British House of Commons, one hundred and fifty-six years ago, used the following remarkable language:

"That Africa, which is not now more fruitful of monsters, than it was once for excellently wise and learned men, — that Africa, which formerly afforded us our *Clemens*, our *Origen*, our *Tertullian*, our *Cyprian*, our *Augustine*, and many other extraordinary lights in the Church of God, — that famous Africa, in whose soil Christianity did thrive so prodigiously, and could boast of so many flourishing churches, — alas! is now a wilderness. ' The wild boars have broken into the vineyard, and ate it up, and it brings forth nothing but briers and thorns,' to use the words of the prophet."

* Quoted by Buxton, p. 228.

tiny, which finally awarded the destiny of sacrifice or bondage ; few or none being left behind to mourn over their slaughtered friends, or the catastrophe of their unhappy country."

The state of a district exempt from the terrors of the slave trade, and then again under their influence, is given by Mr. Randall, who was at St. Louis, on the Senegal, from 1813 to 1817 : " At that time the place was in the possession of the English, and the surrounding population were led to believe that the slave trade was irrevocably abolished ; they, in consequence, betook themselves to cultivating the land, and every available piece of ground was under tillage.   The people passed from one village to another without arms, and without fear, and every thing wore an air of contentment."

Mr. Randall was there again when the place was in the possession of France, " and then," he says, " the slave trade had revived all its horrors. Vessels were lying in the river to receive cargoes of human flesh ; the country was laid waste ; not a vestige of cultivation was to be seen, and no one dared to leave the limits of his village without the most ample means of protection."

It is a significant fact, that while reading of the cruelties of the natives to shipwrecked seamen, we find the people of the same districts, described two hundred years before, as being " unwilling to do injury to any, especially to strangers," and as being " a gentle and loving people."   But under the influence of the slave trade, kindness has given place to a deadly revenge, the spirit of hospitality has yielded to the spirit of war and bloodshed, peaceful neighborhoods have been converted into hostile armies, and there has grown up a fearful indifference to human sufferings and human life.

It is heart-sickening to read of hundreds of human beings offered in the sacrifices of idolatrous worship, and other hundreds put to death, in various ways, for the amusement of a chief or a king.

In 1836, Mr. Girard says that he was at the king's fête at Dahomey, when about five or six hundred of his subjects were sacrificed for his recreation. Some were decapitated, others were precipitated from a lofty fortress, and transfixed on bayonets prepared to receive them; — and all this merely for amusement." *

At the death of a king, immense numbers were sacrificed, and in the most frightful and barbarous manner. "On such an occasion," says Mr. Buxton, "the brothers, sons, and nephews of the king, affecting temporary insanity, burst forth with their muskets, and fire promiscuously among the crowd; even a man of rank, if they meet him, is their victim; nor is their murder of him, or any other, on such an occasion, visited or prevented; the scene can hardly be imagined. I was assured by several, that the custom for Sai Quammie was repeated weekly for three months, and that two hundred

* Colonization Herald, July, 1837.

slaves were sacrificed, and twenty-five barrels of powder fired each time. But the custom for the king's mother, the regent of the kingdom during the invasion of Fantee, is the most celebrated. The king himself devoted three thousand victims, upwards of two thousand of whom were Fantee prisoners. Five of the largest places furnished one hundred victims, and twenty barrels of powder each; and most of the smaller towns, ten victims, and two barrels of powder each."

Mr. Dupries relates many instances of the most atrocious cruelty. As an instance of the bloody customs of Ashantee, he tells us that the king, previous to entering upon the campaign against Gaman, sacrificed "thirty-two males and eighteen females, as an expiatory offering to his gods;" but the answers from the priests being deemed by the council as still devoid of inspiration, the king was induced to "*make a custom*," at the sepulchers of his ancestors, where many hundreds bled. On the conclusion of the war, 2000 prisoners were slaughtered, in honor of the shades of departed kings and heroes."

The existence of these bloody customs is confirmed by the Rev. Thomas B. Freeman,* Wesleyan missionary to Africa, who was an eyewitness to many scenes of horror. Visiting Ashantee in February, 1839, he writes : "Last night a sister of Ko-

* For an interesting account of the condition of the Africans, see "A History of the Wesleyan Missions on the Western Coast of Africa," by William Fox, upwards of ten years a missionary on the Gambia. London, 1851.

michi died, after a long sickness. Her death was announced by the firing of muskets, and the mourners going about the streets. As I walked out in the morning, I saw the mangled corpse of a poor female slave, who had been beheaded during the night, lying in the public street. . . . In the course of the day, I saw groups of the natives dancing around this victim of superstitious cruelty, with numerous frantic gestures, who seemed to be in the zenith of their happiness."

On arriving at Coomassie, Mr. Freeman again witnessed similar scenes of darkness. "Throughout the day," he writes, "I heard the horrid sound of the death drum, and was told in the evening that about twenty-five human beings had been sacrificed, some in the town, and some in the surrounding villages; the heads of those killed in the villages being brought into the town in baskets. I fear that there will be more of this awful work to-morrow."

Again visiting the capital of Ashantee in December, 1841, he says: "In the afternoon I heard that a chief had died, and that three human sacrifices had been made in the town. The mangled victims were left in the street as usual. O God, have mercy upon this benighted people! I saw a lad near my lodgings, who is one of the king's executioners. He had decapitated a poor victim that morning. He appeared to be from sixteen to eighteen years of age. I asked him how many persons he had executed. He answered, 'eighty.' Oh, awful fact! Eighty immortal spirits hurried into the eternal world, by the hands of a boy under eighteen years of age, and he only one of a large number engaged in the same dreadful employment!"

Similar instances of superstition and cruelty are related by the Rev. George Chapman, writing from Coomassie, under date of January 2d, 1844, the Rev. Henry Wharton, another Wesleyan missionary, stationed in Ashantee, in 1846-7, and by the missionaries sent out by other denominations of Christians.

But I need not add to this dark catalogue of revolting crimes. Enough has been said to give a faint idea of the degraded condition of millions of our fellow-men upon the continent of Africa. For more extended accounts, in addition to the works already alluded to, I would refer the reader to the writings of Mungo Park, Bosman, Bowdich, Gray, Landers, and to the letters and journals of our missionaries.

The facts that we have stated are but specimens of the multitudes on record, many of which are more revolting than those which we have adduced.

Gladly would we avoid even an allusion that would excite a painful emotion, but the evils of this accursed trade, and its blighting influence on Africa, ought to be considered, particularly at the present time, by every American citizen. And, notwithstanding all that has been written, the half of the horrors of the system has not been told. There is an unwritten history of the superstitions and cruelties of Africa, known only to the unfortunate sufferers, and to God, "whose justice can not always sleep."

But we need not be understood as arguing that all the evils existing in Africa are caused by the slave trade. Heathenism has done its work there, as well as in other benighted nations, and slavery existed among the people long before the slave trade was opened. In some parts of the continent it is in a mild form; in others it is as severe as in some of our Southern States. The privileges of the masters to abuse their slaves, without redress, are very similar in both countries.*

But it is the opinion of missionaries who have labored in Africa, that the misery of the people has

* "*The master may, at his discretion, inflict any species of punishment upon the person of his slave.*" — *Stroud*, p. 35.

Even for the murder of a slave, the murderer, in several States, is subject only to a fine; and if the slave die under MODERATE CORRECTION, the master is fully acquitted! A law was passed to this effect, in North Carolina, in 1798. It closes thus: "Provided always, this act shall not extend to a person killing a slave outlawed, &c., or *to any slave in the act of resistance to his lawful owner*, or to any slave DYING UNDER MODERATE CORRECTION."

"A slave is one who is in the power of his master to whom he belongs. The master may sell him, dispose of his person, his industry, and his labor. He can do nothing, possess nothing, nor acquire any thing but what belongs to his master." — *Civil Code of Louisiana.*

"The condition of slaves in this country is analogous to that of the ancient Greeks and Romans, and not that of the feudal times. They are generally considered not as persons but as things. They can be sold or transferred, as *goods* or personal estate; they are held to be *pro nullis, pro mortuis*. By the civil law, slaves could not take property by descent or purchase; and I apprehend this to be the law of this country." — *Dess. Rep. IV.* 266. *South Carolina.*

been fearfully augmented by the slave trade, and in some localities, as we have shown, thriving settlements have been changed into a howling wilderness.

Have we not, as a people, a Christian duty to discharge to that unfortunate and suffering people? Is it not time that we arouse ourselves to the great work of Christianizing them, and saving coming generations from the awful calamities that have been suffered in the past?

Let the earnest, stirring words of the devoted missionary, William Fox, that come to us from that benighted land, be sounded through the length and breadth of America.

" Surely, ' the voice of our brother's blood crieth ' against us ' from the ground.' Yes, the sands of Africa, saturated with the life's blood of tens of thousands who have been slain in the seizure, cry against us from the ground; the deserts, and the trackless forests, strewed with the skulls and bones of thousands who have sickened and died in the march to the coast, cry against us from the ground; the prison-houses and the slave-barracoons, planted along the skirts of the coast, on the borders of the Atlantic, crammed with hundreds of negroes who have survived the deadly march, promiscuously thrown together, with shackles on their legs, half perished with hunger, — these cry against us from the ground. And now that the black hull of the rakish vessel is approaching the coast, and these prisoners are liberated, — liberated only to be more closely packed on board the slaver, — Oh, what bitter lamentations, what multitude of voices cry out against us! The winds and the waves, the mighty surge on the beach, join in the melancholy chorus; and the scores of negroes, who are often swamped and

drowned in their passage to the slave ships, and whose
bodies are washed ashore by the swelling tide, once more
cry against us.   But the bitter cries that are heard on board
those floating tombs of gasping humanity on the mighty
deep, by the hundreds who are starved below the decks, and
the sum total of misery endured by those who live to reach
the opposite continent, are known only to God himself!"

    Formed with the same capacity of pain,
The same desire of pleasure and of ease,
Why feels not man for man ?   When nature shrinks
From the slight puncture of an insect's sting,
Faints, if not screened from sultry suns, and pines
Beneath the hardship of an hour's delay
Of needful nutriment; — when Liberty
Is prized so dearly, that the slightest breath
That ruffles but her mantle, can awake
To arm unwarlike nations, and can rouse
Confed'rate states to vindicate her claims: —
How shall the suff'rer man his fellow doom
To ills he mourns or spurns at; tear with stripes
His quiv'ring flesh; with hunger and with thirst
Waste his emaciate frame; in ceaseless toils
Exhaust his vital powers; and bind his limbs
In galling chains!   Shall he, whose fragile form
Demands continual blessings to support
Its complicated texture, air, and food,
Raiment, alternate rest, and kindly skies,
And healthful seasons, dare with impious voice
To ask those mercies, whilst his selfish aim
Arrests the general freedom of their course,
And, gratified beyond his utmost wish,
Debars another from the bounteous store !
                    Roscoe's Wrongs of Africa.

CHAPTER IV.

EFFORTS TO ABOLISH THE SLAVE TRADE.

Leviticus xxv. 10. And ye shall hallow the fiftieth year, and proclaim liberty throughout *all* the land, unto all the inhabitants thereof; it shall be a jubilee unto you ; and ye shall return every man unto his possession, and ye shall return every man unto his family.

> O Liberty ! thou goddess heavenly bright,
> Profuse of bliss, and pregnant with delight !
> Eternal pleasures in thy presence reign,
> And smiling Plenty leads thy wanton train ;
> Eased of her load, Subjection grows more light,
> And poverty looks cheerful in thy sight ;
> Thou mak'st the gloomy face of Nature gay,
> Giv'st beauty to the sun, and pleasure to the day.
>
> JOSEPH ADDISON.

THE slave trade having been tolerated for over two centuries, at length public attention in England and America was aroused to its dreadful evils.

Among the earliest and most zealous advocates of the abolition of this traffic were the members of the society of Friends, whose founder, George Fox, solemnly protested against it, as utterly indefensible. As early as 1668, the celebrated William Penn denounced the trade as impolitic, unchristian, and cruel. In 1696 the subject was introduced at the annual meeting of the Society, and gradually an

interest was awakened, until, at the yearly meeting
in London, in 1727, it was resolved, "That the im
porting of negroes was cruel and unjust, and was
therefore, severely censured by the meeting." In
1760, they went farther, and resolved to exclude
from their Society all who participated in the iniqui
tous traffic.

One of the first instances on record of a voluntary
surrender of slave property, was by a Mr. Mifflin, a
Friend, who, on inheriting forty slaves from his
father, gave them their liberty.*

But the Friends were not alone in their noble
efforts to crush this iniquity. Eminent divines and
statesmen entered the field against the traffic. The
Rev. Morgan Godwyn, of the Church of England,
published the first treatise directly bearing upon the
subject, entitled "The Negro's and Indian's Advocate," which he dedicated to the Archbishop of Can-
terbury. He had witnessed the cruel treatment of
the slaves in the Island of Barbadoes, and he fear-
lessly uttered his sentiments concerning the oppressors.

About the same time, the devoted Richard Bax-
ter pleaded with fervor and eloquence for the rights
of the African. In his "Christian Directory," he
used language, which, if employed in this sensitive
age and nation, would certainly expose him to the
charge of fanaticism. He said that, "those who go

---

* Condensed from "Fox's History of Missions in Africa, and
Account of the Slave Trade."

ut as pirates, and take any poor Africans, and
eople of another land, who never forfeited life or lib-
rty, and make them slaves, or sell them, are the worst
f robbers, and ought to be considered as the com-
non enemies of mankind; and that they who buy
hem, and use them as mere beasts of burden, for
heir own convenience, regardless of their spiritual
velfare, are fitter to be called demons than Chris-
ians."

Many other treatises and tracts were published,
vhich took the strongest ground against the traffic.
\s early as 1739, the eloquent preacher of righteous-
less, Rev. George Whitefield, while in America,
iddressed a letter to the settlers in districts where
slavery existed, which produced a marked effect;
ind to the close of life, he pleaded for the oppressed
vith great success. The following is an extract
rom said letter:

"As I lately passed through your provinces in my way
iither, I was sensibly touched with a fellow-feeling for the
niseries of the poor negroes. Whether it be lawful for
Christians to buy slaves, and thereby encourage the nations
rom whom they are bought to be at perpetual war with
ach other, I shall not take upon me to determine. Sure I
im it is sinful, when they have bought them, to use them as
oad as though they were brutes, — nay, worse; and what-
ver particular exceptions there may be, (as I would charit-
ibly hope there are some,) I fear the generality of you who
own negroes are liable to such a charge; for your slaves, I
oelieve, work as hard, if not harder, than the horses whereon

you ride. These, after they have done their work, are fed and taken proper care of; but many negroes, when wearied with labor in your plantations, have been obliged to grind their corn after their return home. Your dogs are caressed and fondled at your table, but your slaves, who are frequently styled dogs or beasts, have not an equal privilege. They are scarce permitted to pick up the crumbs which fall from their master's table. Not to mention what numbers have been given up to the inhuman usage of cruel task-masters, who, by their unrelenting scourges, have ploughed their backs, and made long furrows, and at length brought them even unto death. When passing along, I have viewed your plantations cleared and cultivated, many spacious houses built, and the owners of them faring sumptuously every day, my blood has frequently almost run cold within me, to consider how many of your slaves had neither convenient food to eat, nor proper raiment to put on, notwithstanding most of the comforts you enjoy were solely owing to their indefatigable labors." — *Letter to the inhabitants of Maryland, Virginia, North and South Carolina, 1739.*

Few men felt more keenly the wrongs of the slave trade than the eminent John Wesley, a name that should be an authority in this land, south and north. In 1774, he published his " Thoughts upon Slavery," and burning thoughts they are. We give two as specimens. Would that our brethren of the Methodist church would publish the whole tract, and circulate it over the country. He says :

" V. I add a few words to those who are more immediately concerned.

" 1. *To Traders.*—You have torn away children from their

arents, and parents from their children; husbands from their
ives; wives from their beloved husbands; brethren and sisters
om each other. You have dragged them who have never
one you any wrong, in chains, and forced them into the
llest slavery, never to end but with life ; such slavery as is
ot found among the Turks in Algiers, nor among the
eathens in America. You induce the villain to steal, rob,
urder men, women, and children, without number, by pay-
ıg him for his execrable labor. It is all your act and deed.
ı your conscience quite reconciled to this ? Does it never
eproach you at all ? Has gold entirely blinded your eyes,
ıd stupefied your heart? Can you see, can you *feel* no
ırm therein ? Is it doing as you would be done to ?
[ake the case your own. 'Master,' said a slave at Liver-
)ol, to the merchant that owned him, ' what if some of my
)untrymen were to come here, and take away mistress, and
'ommy, and Billy, and carry them into our country, and
ıake them slaves, how would you like it ? ' His answer
as worthy of a man : ' I will never buy a slave more while
live.' Let his resolution be yours. Have no more any
ırt in this detestable business. Instantly leave it to those
nfeeling wretches ' who laugh at human nature and com-
ıssion.' Be you a man ; not a wolf, a devourer of the
uman species. Be merciful, that you may obtain mercy.

" Is there a God ? You know there is. Is he a just God ?
'hen there must be a state of retribution ; a state wherein
ıe just God will reward every man according to his works.
'hen what reward will he render to *you?* Oh, think be-
mes, before you drop into eternity ! Think now. ' He
ıall have judgment without mercy that hath showed no
ıercy.' Are you a *man ?* Then you should have a human
eart. But have you, indeed ? What is your heart made
f ? Is there no such principle as compassion there ? Do

you never feel another's pain ? Have you no sympathy ? no sense of human woe ? no pity for the miserable ? When you saw the streaming eyes, the heaving breasts, the bleeding sides, and the tortured limbs of your fellow-creatures, were you a stone, or a brute ? Did you look upon them with the eyes of a tiger ? Had you no relenting ? Did not one tear drop from your eye, one sigh escape from your breast ? Do you feel no relenting now ? If you do not, you must go on till the measure of your iniquities is full. Then will the great God deal with you, as you have dealt with them, and require all their blood at your hands. At that day it shall be more tolerable for Sodom and Gomorrah than for you. But if your heart does relent, resolve, God being your helper, to escape with your life. Regard not money ! All that a man hath, will he give for his life. Whatever you lose, lose not your soul; nothing can countervail that loss. Immediately quit the horrid trade. At all events, be an honest man.

"2. *To Slaveholders.* — This equally concerns all slave-holders, of whatever rank and degree ; seeing *men-buyers are exactly on a level with men-stealers !* 'Indeed,' you say, ' I pay honestly for my goods, and I am not concerned to know how they are come by.' Nay, but you are ; you are deeply concerned to know they are honestly come by : otherwise you are partaker with a thief, and are not a jot honester than he. But you know they are not honestly come by ; you know they are procured by means *nothing near so innocent as picking pockets, house-breaking, or robbery upon the highway.* You know they are procured by a deliberate species of more complicated villainy, of fraud, robbery, and murder, than was ever practiced by Mohammedans or Pagans ; in particular, by murders of all kinds ; by the blood of the innocent poured upon the ground like water. Now it is *your* money that pays the African butcher. *You*, therefore, are principally guilty of all these frauds, robberies, and murders. *You* are the spring that puts all the rest in motion. They would not stir a step without *you :* therefore, the blood of all these wretches who die before their time lies upon *your* head. ' The blood of thy brother crieth against thee from the earth.' Oh! whatever it costs, put a stop to its cry before it be too late ; instantly, at any price, were it the half of your goods, deliver thyself from blood guiltiness! *Thy hands, thy bed, thy furniture, thy house, and thy lands, at present are stained with blood.* Surely it is enough ; accumulate no more guilt ; spill no more the blood of the innocent. Do not hire another to shed blood ; do not pay him for doing it. Whether you are a Christian or not, show yourself a man. Be not more savage than a lion or a bear ! "

Similar earnest appeals were made by other distinguished Christians and philanthropists. In 1785, Thomas Clarkson took the field against the traffic in human beings, and devoted to the sacred cause of human rights all the energies of his intellect, and sympathies of his heart.

While pursuing his studies at Cambridge University, "The Slave Trade" was given to him as a theme for a prize essay. Having, the year before, gained the first prize for a Latin dissertation, he was anxious to sustain his literary reputation, and secure, if possible, fresh laurels. He entered upon the investigation with great ardor; visited London, and read with avidity works bearing upon the subject. The horrible facts that passed in review before him so deeply affected his mind, that he lost sight of the

honors of the university, in the intensity of his
desire to redress the wrongs of Africa. "It is impossible," he says, in his "History of Slavery," "to
imagine the severe anguish which the composition
of this essay cost me. All the pleasure that I had
promised myself from the contest, was exchanged for
pain, by the astounding facts that were now continually before me. It was one gloomy subject, from
morning till night. In the day, I was agitated and
uneasy; in the night I had little or no rest. I was
so overwhelmed with grief, that I sometimes never
closed my eyes during the whole night; and I no
longer regarded my essay as a mere trial for literary
distinction. My great desire now was to produce a
work that should call forth a vigorous public effort
to redress the wrongs of injured Africa."

Under the influence of this desire, and with his
intellectual powers thoroughly aroused and concen-
trated upon the theme, he produced an essay that
not only won the highest prize, but touched a chord
in the English heart that has not ceased to vibrate
to this hour. And the great secret of his success in
this, and in his subsequent efforts, was the fact, that
he gave his whole soul to the work. He thus describes his feelings while on his way to London, after
having read the essay at the university: "During
my journey, the melancholy subject was not a moment absent from my thoughts. I occasionally
stopped my horse, dismounted, and walked. I tried
frequently to persuade myself that the statements

in my essay could not be true. But the more I reflected on the authorities on which they were founded, the more constrained was I to give them credit. I sat down, disconsolate, on the turf by the road-side; and here it forcibly occurred to me, that if the statements that I had made were facts, it was high time that something should be done to put an end to such cruelties."

These convictions increased, rather than diminished, in the noble-hearted youth, and he felt that to accomplish any thing, he must give himself wholly to the work. Upon this point he consulted the ardent friends of freedom; and after mature deliberation, and a careful survey of the difficulties of the undertaking, he resolved to abandon all other pursuits, and give his life to the abolition of the slave trade and slavery.

The electric influence of his decision was at once felt upon others;—it increased their confidence, and fired their zeal. Sir Charles Middleton, M. P., Dr. Porteus, and Lord Scarsdale, both members of the House of Lords; Granville Sharp, J. Phillips Ramsay, and the united Society of Friends,—all rallied to his support. They knew the sacrifices that he had made, the brilliant prospects for usefulness and distinction in the church that he had renounced, and the struggles through which his mind had passed,— and they applauded the decision. They were impressed with his sincerity, his ardor, and his readiness to obey the divine will in the matter. Nor was he without encouragement from a higher source. He declared that he pledged himself to the task, "not because I saw any reasonable prospect of success in my new undertaking, but in obedience, I believe, to a higher power. And I can say, that both at the moment of this resolution, and for some time afterwards, I had more sublime and happy feelings than at any former period of my life."

In the prosecution of his work, Clarkson visited every person in London and the vicinity, who had been connected with the slave trade, or who had visited Africa; and he also inspected the slave ships, and informed himself upon every point touching the iniquity he had grappled with. The startling facts which he had accumulated, aroused many to the enormity of the evil, and especially Mr. Wilberforce, who at once coöperated with Mr. Clarkson, and through life rendered his name illustrious by his devotion to the cause of human liberty.

Soon after, a committee of twelve gentlemen was formed for the purpose of bringing the evils of slavery more fully before the British nation, and to organize a society for its entire abolition. At the head of this committee stood Granville Sharp, whom Clarkson justly styled, "the father of the cause in England." To promote their object, public meetings were held, treatises, showing the evils of the slave trade, were widely circulated, and many petitions were sent to Parliament, praying for the abolition of the traffic.

The history of the efforts made to secure the action of Parliament, though deeply interesting and instructive, our limits will not allow us to give in its details.* It is sufficient to state that the subject was introduced into the House of Commons in 1788, by Mr. Pitt, who proposed that the slave trade should be investigated at the next sessions. He was ably supported by Mr. Fox, Mr. Burke, Sir. W. Dolben, and others, and the motion passed unanimously.

Another measure, on the 22d of May, was proposed by Sir W. Dolben, which excited alarm among the traders in Liverpool and Bristol. It was that the number of slaves brought in a vessel should be in proportion to its tonnage. This the pro-slavery party were determined to resist, and they obtained leave to be heard by counsel before the House in their defense. But thus early, British philanthropy triumphed, and the motion passed by a large majority.

As the friends of humanity pushed their measures,† opposition was of course excited, and the advocates of the traffic succeeded in defeating motion after motion, until 1804, when the abolition bill was carried through the House of Commons. It was, how-

---

* For a full account of these efforts, see " Clarkson's History of the Abolition of the Slave Trade."

† In April, 1792, no less than five hundred and seventeen petitions against the slave trade had been laid before Parliament.

ever, thrown out by the House of Lords. and the next year it was lost in the Commons.

The people now rose in their strength, and pulpits and presses thundered their anathemas against the great national disgrace. The indefatigable Clarkson provided himself with fresh materials, that he might be ready to meet the arguments of his opponents, convince the doubting, and especially to influence the House of Lords to a right decision.

The hour of victory was at hand. On the 10th of June, 1806, the following resolution was moved in both houses: "That this House, considering the African Slave Trade to be contrary to the principles of justice, humanity, and sound policy, will, with all practicable expedition, take effectual measures for the abolition of said trade, in such manner, and at such period, as may be deemed advisable."

In a lengthy debate, the resolution was opposed, on the ground that it might be injurious to the trade of Liverpool; affect unfavorably the planters, and gentlemen engaged in the traffic; reduce the revenue of the country; be a reflection upon the characters of their ancestors, who established the business, and deprive the Africans themselves of the advantages of a residence in the West Indies; all of which arguments were scattered to the wind by the invincible logic of the defenders of the resolution. The Bishop of St. Asaph, in the upper House, remarked, on commencing his speech, "My lords, I can not but assent to every part of the resolution

ow before your lordships, at any season of the year,
r any day of the year, or any hour of the day."

The idea of supporting the traffic on account of
ts antiquity, was ably refuted by the declaration
hat any villainy which had existed since Cain mur-
lered his brother, might be sustained on the same
ground.

The assertion that the Scriptures countenanced
he traffic, was denounced as " one of the greatest
ibels that was ever published against the Christian
eligion." The other objections were disposed of
very easily, and the resolution passed by a majority
f ninety-nine in the House of Commons, and
wenty-one in the House of Lords.

The next year a bill was introduced, entitled " An
ct for the abolition of the slave trade," which also
assed by large majorities. The friends of humanity
vere now exultant. The heroes of the mighty rev-
lution which had been achieved in public sentiment
xchanged congratulations, and expressed their
gratitude to Heaven for so signal a victory.

In the midst of these rejoicings, a deep anxiety
ervaded the kingdom, lest the bill should not
eceive the sanction of the Crown. But just before
he dissolution of the ministry, it was announced
hat the king had given his assent, and the act, in
he usual way, became a law. "Just as the clock
truck twelve, while the sun was shining in its me-
idian splendor, as if to witness the august act, and
o sanction it by its glorious beams, the *magna
harta* of Africa was completed."

Thus the first effectual blow against the slave trade was struck, and the friends of the African believed that the unholy system had received its death-wound. But they did not rightly estimate the strength of human wickedness, and the power of those fiendish passions that were burning in the hearts of corrupt men. They did not see that the lust for gold would continue to seek gratification, at whatever expense of cruelty, and that brutes in human shape would laugh at compassion, sneer at just laws, and spurn the very idea of mercy.

For, what does a man engaged in this traffic know of humanity, justice, or the rights of a fellow man? What does he care for the sufferings of the captive, the shrieks of the agonized mother, the imploring looks and pathetic appeals of the dying slave? With the horrors of the middle passage constantly before him, does his heart relent? Looking down upon the crowded group of miserable, groaning victims of his cupidity, does a tear start in his eye? Throwing overboard the sick, for the sake of the insurance, does he reflect upon the infinite sacrifices he makes to gain a few dollars? A slave trader reflecting! What an absurdity! His conscience and heart moved! He *has* no conscience, — has no heart. Look into the soul of the captain of a slave ship, and what do you see? You need not read the vision of Dante, nor visit afterwards the regions of the lost.

Still the friends of the slave were hopeful, and

fforts were made to secure the coöperation of the
ther European powers, and of the States of Amer-
ca, in the suppression of the traffic. Our country,
owever, had been moving simultaneously with
reat Britain; and, to its honor be it said, it was
he first to prohibit the prosecution of the slave
rade.

As early as 1794,* it was enacted, that no person
n the United States should fit out any vessel for
he purpose of carrying on any traffic in slaves to a
oreign country, or for procuring from any foreign
country the inhabitants thereof, to be disposed of as
laves. In 1800, it was declared to be unlawful for
any citizen of the United States to have property in
any vessel employed in transporting slaves from
one foreign country to another, or to serve on board
such a vessel.

A more stringent law was passed in 1807, to take
effect on the first of January, 1808, declaring that
no one should bring into the United States, or the
territories thereof, from any foreign country, any
negro, mulatto, or person of color, with the intention
of holding him or selling him as a slave; and heavy
penalties were imposed on the violators of this law,

As an evidence of the progress of public sentiment, and the general and deep-seated abhorrence
of the slave trade in the American mind at that
time, the traffic, in 1820, was pronounced *piracy*, and

* Encyclopædia Americana, vol. xi. p. 433.

the guilty participators in the crime were adjudged
worthy of death. It was enacted:

"If any citizen of the United States, being of the crew, or
ship's company of any foreign ship or vessel engaged in the
slave trade, or any person whatever, being of the crew or
ship's company of any ship or vessel owned in the whole, or
navigated for, or in behalf of, any citizen or citizens of the
United States, shall land from any such ship or vessel, and
on any foreign shore seize any negro or mulatto, not held to
service or labor by the laws of either of the States or Territories of the United States, with intent to make such negro or
mulatto a slave, or shall decoy, or forcibly bring, or carry, or
shall receive such negro or mulatto on board any such ship
or vessel, with intent as aforesaid, such citizen or person
shall be adjudged a PIRATE, and on conviction thereof, before
the Circuit Court of the United States, for the district
wherein he may be brought or found, SHALL SUFFER DEATH."

At that period, and as far back as the time when
the United States Constitution was adopted, the
hostility to slavery was national, and the pro-slavery
feeling was local, and limited to a comparatively
small portion of the people. We might fill volumes
with the testimony of the great and good men of
that day, which contributed to the formation of the
public opinion that called for the enactment of
the laws to which we have referred.

In addition to the opinions of Washington, Jefferson, Patrick Henry, Jay, and Hamilton, already
quoted, let me call the reader's attention to the sen-

ents of others, whose influence and services are
orporated in the history of the republic.

Benjamin Franklin, according to Steuben's ac-
nt, (see Life of Franklin, by William Temple
anklin,) was President of the Pennsylvania So-
ty for Promoting the Abolition of Slavery, and as
ch signed the memorial that was presented to the
use of Representatives of the United States, on
e 12th of February, 1789, praying that body to
ert, to their fullest extent, the power vested in
em by the Constitution, in discouraging the traffic
human flesh.   In the memorial the system of sla-
ry is condemned in the strongest language, and it
ses with a most touching and earnest appeal to
e Senate and House of Representatives of the
nited States, " to devise means for removing this
consistency from the character of the American
ople, and to step to the very verge of the power
sted in them for discouraging every species of
affic in the persons of our fellow men."

Other memorials were sent in 1791.   In the
emorial from Connecticut it is stated :

" That the whole system of African slavery is unjust in its
ture, impolitic in its principles, and in its consequences
inous to the industry and enterprise of the citizens of
ese States."

The memorialists from Pennsylvania say :

" We wish not to trespass on your time by referring to the
fferent declarations made by Congress, *on the inalienable*

right of all men to equal liberty, neither would we attempt, in this place, to point out the inconsistency of extending freedom to a part only of the human race."

Hear, also, the voice that sixty years ago was uttered by Virginia:

"Your memorialists, believing that 'righteousness exalteth a nation,' and that slavery is not only an odious degradation, but *an outrageous violation of one of the most essential rights of human nature*, and utterly repugnant to the precepts of the gospel, which breathes 'peace on earth, and good will to men,' lament that a practice so inconsistent with true policy, and the *inalienable rights of men*, should subsist in an enlightened age, and among a people *professing that all mankind are by nature equally entitled* to freedom."

These memorials were not only read in the House of Representatives, but were referred to a select committee.

James Monroe, in a speech pronounced in the Virginia Convention, said:

"We have found that this evil has preyed upon the very vitals of the Union, and has been prejudicial to all the States in which it has existed."

The views of Samuel Adams may be learned from the following extract:

"His principles on the subject of human rights carried him beyond the narrow limits which many loud asserters of their own liberty have prescribed to themselves, to the recognition of this right in every human being. One day the wife

Ir: Adams returning home, informed her husband that a
nd had made her a present of a female slave. Mr.
ams replied, in a firm, decided manner: *"She may come,
not as a slave, for a slave can not live in my house, if she
es, she must come free.'* She came, and took her free
de with the family of this great champion of American
rty, and there she continued free, and there she died
.." — *Rev. Mr. Allen, Uxbridge, Mass.*

At a meeting in Darien, Georgia, in 1775, the fol-
ving resolution was put forth :

To show the world that we are not influenced by any
tracted or interested motives, but by a general philan-
opy for all mankind, of whatever climate, language, or
uplexion, *we hereby declare our disapprobation and abhor-
ce of the unnatural practice of slavery,* (however the
cultivated state of the country, or other specious argu-
nts, may plead for it ;) *a practice founded in injustice and
elty, and highly dangerous to our liberties as well as lives,
asing part of our fellow creatures below men, and corrupt-
the virtue and morals of the rest,* and laying the basis of
it liberty we contend for, and which we pray the Al-
ghty to continue to the latest posterity, upon a very wrong
ndation. We therefore resolve, at all times to use our
nost endeavors for the manumission of our slaves in this
ony, upon the most safe and equitable footing for the
sters and themselves." — *Am. Archives,* 4th *Series, Vol. I.,*
1135.

The patriotic, high-minded, and eloquent Wil-
m Pinkney, in a speech in the Maryland House
Delegates, in 1789, said :

" Eternal infamy awaits the abandoned miscreants, whos
selfish souls could ever prompt them to rob unhappy Afric
of her sons, and freight them hither by thousands, to poiso
the fair Eden of Liberty with the rank weed of individua
bondage! Nor is it more to the credit of our ancestors, tha
they did not command these savage spoilers to bear the
hateful cargo to another shore, where the shrine of freedo
knew no votaries, and every purchaser would at once
both a master and a slave.

" In the dawn of time, when the rough feelings of ba
barism had not experienced the softening touches of refine
ment, such an unprincipled prostration of the inherent righ
of human nature would have needed the gloss of an apology
but to the everlasting reproach of Maryland, be it said, tha
when her citizens rivaled the nation from whence they em
grated, in the knowledge of moral principles, and an enth
siasm in the cause of general freedom, they stooped to b
come the purchasers of their fellow creatures, and to intr
duce an hereditary bondage into the bosom of their countr
which should widen with every successive generation.

" For my own part, I would willingly draw the veil
oblivion over this disgusting scene of iniquity, but that th
present abject state of those who are descended from thes
kidnapped sufferers, perpetually brings it forward to th
memory.

" But wherefore should we confine the edge of censure
our ancestors, or those from whom they purchased? A
not we *equally guilty?* *They* strewed around the seeds
slavery, — *we* cherish and sustain the growth. *They* intr
duced the system, — *we* enlarge, invigorate, and confirm
Yes, let it be handed down to posterity, that the people
Maryland, who could fly to arms with the promptitude
Roman citizens, when the hand of oppression was lifted

gainst themselves; who could behold their country deso-
ated, and their citizens slaughtered; who could brave, with
ushaken firmness, every calamity of war, before they would
ibmit to the smallest infringement of their rights, — that
iis very people could yet see thousands of their fellow
reatures, within the limits of their territory, bending be-
eath an unnatural yoke; and, instead of being assiduous to
estroy their shackles, anxious to immortalize their duration,
ı that a nation of slaves might for ever exist in a country
·here freedom is its boast."

The whole speech is one of irresistible force, noble
entiment, and burning eloquence.

The style in which the House of Representatives
·as addressed at that period, may be learned from
he letter of Warner Mifflin, dated in Kent County,
)elaware, 2d of 1st month, 1793. He said:

"But whether you will hear or forbear, I think it my duty
ı tell you plainly, that I believe that the blood of the slain,
nd the oppression exercised in Africa, promoted by Amer-
:ans, and in this country also, will stick to the skirts of
very individual of your body, who exercise the powers of
ıgislation, and do not exert their talents to clear themselves
f this abomination, when they shall be arraigned before the
·emendous bar of the judgment-seat of Him who will not
ıil to do right, in rendering unto every man his due; even
Iim who early declared, 'at the hand of every man's
rother will I require the life of man;' before whom the
atural black skin of the body will never occasion such
egradation. I desire to approach you with proper and due
espect, in the temper of a Christian, and the firmness of a
eteran American freeman, to plead the cause of injured

innocence, and open my mouth for my oppressed brethren, who can not open theirs for themselves.. . . The almost daily accounts I have of the inhumanity perpetrated in these States, on this race of men, distresses me night and day, and brings the subject of the slave trade with more pressure on my spirit; and I believe I feel a measure of the same obligation that the prophet did when he was ordered to 'cry aloud, spare not; lift up thy voice like a trumpet, and show my people their transgressions, and the house of Jacob their sins.' And here I think I can show that our nation is revolting from the law of God, the law of reason and humanity, and the just principles of government, and with rapid strides establishing tyranny and oppression."

When the subject of continuing or abolishing the slave trade was before the Convention called to frame the Constitution of these United States, some of the members expressed very boldly and fully their views upon the whole slavery question. I will give a few extracts, as reported by Mr. Yates, (pp. 64–67:)

" It was said that we had just assumed a place among independent nations, in consequence of our opposition to the attempts of Great Britain to enslave us, that this opposition was grounded upon the preservation of those rights to which God and nature had entitled us, not in particular, but in common with all the rest of mankind. That we had appealed to the Supreme Being for his assistance as a *God of freedom ;* who could not but approve our efforts to preserve the rights which he had thus imparted to his creatures; that now, when we scarcely had risen from our knees, from supplicating his aid and protection — in forming our government over a free people, a government formed pretendedly on the

rinciples of liberty, and for its preservation, — in that gov-
:nment to have a provision, not only putting it out of its
)wer to restrain and prevent the slave trade, even encour-
;ing that most infamous traffic, by giving the States power
id union, in proportion as they cruelly and wantonly sport
ith the rights of their fellow creatures, ought to be consid-
:ed as a solemn mockery of, and insult to, that God whose
rotection we then implored, and could not fail to hold us up
ı detestation, and render us contemptible to every true
iend of liberty in the world. . . . . That, on the contrary,
e ought rather to prohibit, expressly, in our Constitution,
ıe further importation of slaves; and to authorize the gen-
:al government, from time to time, to make such regula-
ons as should be thought advantageous, for the gradual
)olition of slavery and the emancipation of the slaves which
:e already in the States.

" That slavery is inconsistent with the genius of republi-
ınism, and has a tendency to destroy those principles on
hich it is supported, as it lessens the sense of the equal
ghts of mankind, and habituates us to tyranny and oppres-
on. It was further urged, that by this system of govern-
ıent, every State is to be protected both from foreign inva-
ons and from domestic insurrections; that from this consid-
ration, it was of the utmost importance it should have a
)wer to restrain the importation of slaves, since in propor-
on as the number of slaves was increased in any State, in
ıe same proportion the State is weakened, and exposed to
)reign invasion or domestic insurrection, and by so much
:ss will it be able to protect itself against either, and there-
)re will, by so much the more, want aid from, and be a bur-
en to, the Union."

But I need not multiply testimonies on this point.
Ivery student of American history knows what has

5

been the state of the public mind, in the past, on the question before us.

But the inquiry is made, how far the laws against the slave trade, passed by Great Britain, the United States, and other nations,* were successful in suppressing the traffic.

As we have already intimated, the answer to this question opens a melancholy chapter in the history of human nature. But before entering upon it, we can not but pay a passing tribute to the noble philanthropy of Great Britain, and to the efforts of our ancestors to sweep from the earth the curse of the traffic in human beings.

Whatever may have been the course of England in regard to her other great national interests, we must allow, that in her hostility to slavery and the slave trade, she has been firm, consistent, and self-sacrificing; and deserves the hearty applause of the civilized world. She has grappled with this evil boldly, manfully, as under a solemn consciousness of her obligations to society, and accountability to God. Mistress of the seas, she has struck this infa-

* In 1815, Louis XVIII., by the treaty of Paris, consented to the immediate abolition of the slave trade. Denmark, as early as 1804, declared the trade unlawful. Sweden did the same in 1813, and in 1831 conferred upon the free negroes in the island of St. Bartholomew, all the privileges that the whites enjoyed. Portugal, having received the promise of £300,000 from England, provided for the abolition of the slave trade in 1823. Spain came into the measure in 1820, her citizens having been paid £400,000 by England. On the 24th of December, 1814, the United States engaged, according to the treaty of Ghent, to do all in their power to suppress the traffic. We shall soon see how the promise was fulfilled.

ous traffic from the roll of her commerce. Sovreign of vast territories, she has decreed that no lave shall breathe the air of her realms.

Her diplomatic influence has been used to arouse ther governments to a sense of their duty, and ecure their coöperation in this great work of huanity. For years she has, at great expense, susained her cruisers along the coast of Africa, and ear the West Indies, to break up the vile traffic. he has poured out her money like water, in the ause, having, in 1833, borrowed twenty millions of ounds, to purchase the freedom of slaves in her colnies, and up to 1843, having expended fifteen millions f pounds sterling in payment to foreign governents and courts, to effect the extinction of the lave trade.

Had the other European nations come up to the ork as they ought to have done, and had the good eginning made in America been prosecuted with a erseverance and zeal commensurate with the growth f our national power, and the increase of our eduational and religious privileges, this great wickedess might have been annihilated.

And why has America retrograded? What has hilled her heart, and palsied her energies, and made er pause in the career of fame and glory? What as blinded the eyes of her citizens to their true nterests, corrupted her government, struck dumb he ministers at the altar, and clothed oppression vith such power?

WE have a goodly clime,
  Broad vales and streams we boast,
Our mountain frontiers frown sublime,
  Old Ocean guards our coast;
Suns bless our harvest fair,
  With fervid smile serene,
But a dark shade is gathering there!—
  What can its blackness mean?

We have a birthright proud,
  For our young sons to claim,
An eagle soaring o'er the cloud,
  In freedom and in fame;
We have a scutcheon bright,
  By our dear fathers bought,—
A fearful blot distains its white,
  Who hath such evil wrought?

Our banner o'er the sea
  Looks forth with starry eye,
Emblazoned, glorious, bold, and free,
  A letter on the sky.
What hand, with shameful stain,
  Hath marred its heavenly blue?
The yoke! the fetters! and the chain!
  Say, are these emblems true?

*This day** doth music rare
  Swell through our nation's bound,
But Afric's wailing mingles there,
  And Heaven doth hear the sound!
O God of power! we turn
  In penitence to thee;
Bid our loved land the lesson learn,—
  To bid the slave be free.   Mrs. L. H. Sigourney.
        * Fourth of July.

CHAPTER V.

FAILURE OF MEASURES TO EXTERMINATE THE SLAVE TRADE.

Jeremiah xxxiv. 17. Therefore, thus saith the Lord, Ye have not hearkened unto me, in proclaiming liberty, every one to his brother, and every man to his neighbor : behold, I proclaim a liberty for you, saith the Lord, to the sword, to the pestilence, and to the famine ; and I will make you to be removed into all the kingdoms of the earth.

It is a melancholy and startling fact, that the slave trade is not abolished, but continues, with all its attendant barbarities and unmitigated horrors. Cuba, Brazil, Porto Rico, and the United States, still furnish markets for men whose trade has been pronounced piracy, and whose crimes render them deserving of death. There is more cruelty, and a greater waste of life, than formerly, owing to the smallness of the vessels employed, the scanty provisions furnished, and the haste with which the captives must be taken, in order that the pirates may escape seizure by the armed vessels in pursuit of them.

Mr. Buxton, who is good authority on this point, says :

"It has been proved, by documents which can not be controverted, that for every cargo of slaves shipped towards the end of the last century, two cargoes, or twice the numbers in one cargo, wedged together in a mass of living corruption, are now borne on the waves of the Atlantic; and that the cruelties and horrors of the traffic have been increased and aggravated *by the very efforts we have made for its abolition.* Each individual has more to endure; aggravated suffering reaches multiplied numbers. At the time I am writing, there are at least *twenty thousand human beings* on the Atlantic, exposed to every variety of wretchedness which belongs to the middle passage. . . . I am driven to the sorrowful conviction, that the year from September, 1837, to September, 1838, is distinguished beyond all preceding years for the extent of the trade, for the intensity of its miseries, and for the unusual havoc it makes of human life."

Judge Joseph Story, in his charge to the grand jury of the United States Circuit Court, in Portsmouth, N. H., May term, 1820, after reviewing the laws which have been enacted for the suppression of the slave trade, remarked:

"Under such circumstances, it might well be supposed that the slave trade would, in practice, be extinguished, — that virtuous men would, by their abhorrence, stay its polluted march, and wicked men would be overawed by its potent punishment. But, unfortunately, the case is far otherwise. We have but too many melancholy proofs, from unquestionable sources, that it is still carried on with all the implacable ferocity and insatiable rapacity of former times. Avarice has grown more subtle in its evasion; and watches and seizes its prey with an appetite quickened, rather than uppressed, by its guilty vigils. American citizens are steeped up to their very mouths, (I scarcely use too bold a figure,) in this stream of iniquity. They throng the coasts of Africa, under the stained flags of Spain and Portugal, sometimes selling abroad 'their cargoes of despair,' and sometimes bringing them into some of our southern ports, and there, under the forms of the law, defeating the purposes of the law itself, and legalizing their inhuman but profitable adventures. I wish I could say that New England, and New England men, were free from this deep pollution. But there is some reason to believe that they who drive a loathsome traffic, 'and buy the muscles and the bones of men,' are to be found here also. It is to be hoped the number is small; but our cheeks may well burn with shame while a solitary case is permitted to go unpunished.

"And, gentlemen, how can we justify ourselves, or apologize for an indifference to this subject? Our constitutions of government have declared that all men are born free and equal, and have certain inalienable rights, among which are the right of enjoying their lives, liberties, and property, and of seeking and obtaining their own safety and happiness. May not the miserable African ask, 'Am I not a man, and a brother?' We boast of our noble struggle against the encroachments of tyranny, but do we forget that it assumed the mildest form in which authority ever assailed the rights of its subjects, and yet that there are men among us who think it no wrong to condemn the shivering negro to perpetual slavery?

"We believe in the Christian religion. It commands us to have good will to all men; to love our neighbors as ourselves, and to do unto all men as we would they should do unto us. It declares our accountability to the Supreme God for all our actions, and holds out to us a state of future rewards and punishments, as the sanction by which our conduct is to be regulated. And yet there are men calling themselves Christians, who degrade the negro by ignorance to a level with the brutes, and deprive him of all the consolations of religion. He alone, of all the rational creation, they seem to think, is to be at once accountable for his actions, and yet his actions are not to be at his own disposal, but his mind, his body, and his feelings, are to be sold to perpetual bondage. To me it appears perfectly clear, that the slave trade is equally repugnant to the dictates of reason and religion, and is an offense equally against the laws of God and man."

We shall not undertake the arduous task of fixing the precise amount of guilt that belongs to our nation, for the failure of the efforts to destroy this traffic. The amount of that guilt can not be estimated, — can not be put into language. The indifference that has been manifested towards the evils of the traffic; the toleration of the domestic slave trade, by which the public conscience has been rendered callous; the extension of slave territory, in spite of the solemn remonstrances of the enlightened and patriotic portion of the people; and the refusal of the government to coöperate with the nations of Europe in their humane efforts, have tended to sustain the traffic, and place us in an anomalous position before the world.

After the refusal of the United States, in 1833, to join with England and France for the suppression of the traffic, what encouragement has there been for those governments to renew their applications for coöperation? This shameful refusal is thus referred to in the 128th number of the Edinburgh Review:

"We have, however, to record one instance of positive refusal to our request of accession to these conventions, and that, we grieve to say, comes from the United States of America, — the first nation that, by its statute law, branded the slave trade with the name of piracy. The conduct, moreover, of the President does not appear to have been perfectly candid and ingenuous. There appears to have been delay in returning any answer, and when returned, it seems to have been of an evasive character. In the month of August, 1833, the English and French ministers jointly sent in copies of the recent conventions, and requested the accession of the United States. At the end of March following, seven months afterwards, an answer is returned, which, though certainly not of a favorable character in other respects, yet brings so prominently into view, as the insuperable objection, that the mutual right of search of suspected vessels was to be extended to the shores of the United States, (though we permitted it to American cruisers off the coast of our West Indian colonies,) that Lord Palmerston was naturally led to suppose that the other objections were superable. He, therefore, though aware how much the whole efficiency of the agreement will be impaired, consents to waive that part of it, in accordance with the wishes of the President, and in the earnest hope that he will, in return, make some concessions of feeling or opinion to the wishes of England and France, and to the necessities of a great and holy cause. The final answer, however, is, that under no condition, in no form, and with no restrictions, will the United States enter into any convention or treaty, or make combined

efforts of any sort or kind, with other nations, for the suppression of the trade.   We much mistake the state of public
opinion in the United States, if its government will not find
itself under the necessity of changing this resolution.   The
slave trade will, henceforth, we have little doubt, be carried
on under that flag of freedom; but as in no country, after
our own, have such persevering. efforts for its suppression
been made, by men the most distinguished for goodness, wis-
dom, and eloquence, as in the United States, we can not believe that their flag will long be prostituted to such vile purposes; and either they must combine with other nations, or
they must increase the number and efficiency of their naval
forces on the coast of Africa and elsewhere, and do their work
single-handed.   We say this the more, because the motives
which have actuated the government of the United States
in this refusal, clearly have reference to the words 'right of
search.'   They will not choose to see that this is a mutual
restricted right, effected by convention, strictly guarded by
stipulations for one definite object, and confined in its operations within narrow geographical limits; a right, moreover,
which England and France have accorded to each other,
without derogating from the national honor of either.   If we
are right in our conjecture of the motive, and there is evidence to support us, we must consider that the President
and his ministers have been, in this instance, actuated by a
narrow provincial jealousy, and totally unworthy of a great
and independent nation."

The New York Journal of Commerce, of September, 1835, thus refers to the article under the head of

THE SLAVE TRADE.

" The 128th number of the Edinburgh Review contains an
article on this subject, of more than ordinary interest.   In

1831, a convention was concluded between the governments of England and France, for the more effectual suppression of the slave trade; in furtherance of which object, the two contracting parties agreed to the mutual right of search within certain geographical limits. They moreover covenanted to use their best endeavors, and mutually to aid each other, to induce all the maritime powers to agree to the terms of their convention. The fact that such overtures had been made to some nations has occasionally been hinted at, but the results we have now for the first time learned."

After noticing the reception of the proposition by the other European powers, the Journal of Commerce adds:

" We come now to our own country, the United States. And what shall we say ? What must we say ? What does the truth compel us to say ? Why, that of all the countries appealed to by Great Britain and France on this momentous subject, the United States is the only one which has returned a decided negative. We neither do anything ourselves to put down the accursed traffic, nor afford any facilities to enable others to put it down. Nay, rather, we stand between the slave and his deliverer. We are a drawback, a dead weight on the cause of bleeding humanity. How long shall this shameful apathy continue ? How long shall we, who call ourselves the champions of freedom, close our ears to the groans, and our eyes to the tears and blood, and our hearts to the untold anguish of thousands and tens of thousands who are every year torn from home and friends, and bosom companions, and sold into hopeless bondage, or perish amid the horrors of the ' middle passage ? ' From the shores of bleeding Africa, and from the channels of the deep, from Brazil and from Cuba, echo answers, ' How long ? ' "

Through the valleys, and over the plains of this widely extended country, through the streets of every village, town, and city in the Union; through the churches of America, the halls of legislature, the courts of justice, and the mansions of executive officers, we would reiterate the cry, "How long?" Is the conscience of the nation absolutely dead? Is there no heart to feel, no eye to see the horrors of the traffic, no tongue to speak for the agonized sufferers in the "middle passage?" Shall we go to France and England, to Denmark, Sardinia, and Mexico* to learn humanity?

* Even, unfortunate (!) Mexico, whose condition we so much commiserate, can give us lessons in justice, magnanimity, and humanity. Shall we not send some of our politicians to school there? It will be an economical arrangement, provided they stay long enough.

The following decrees and ordinances are translated from an official compilation, published by authority of the Mexican government.

DECREE OF JULY 13, 1824.
Prohibition of the Commerce and Traffic in Slaves.

The Sovereign General Constituent Congress of the United Mexican States has held it right to decree the following:

1. The commerce and traffic in slaves, proceeding from whatever power, and under whatever flag, is for ever prohibited within the territories of the United Mexican States.

2. The slaves who may be introduced, contrary to the tenor of the preceding article, shall remain free in consequence of treading the Mexican soil.

3. Every vessel, whether national or foreign, in which slaves may be transported and introduced into the Mexican territories, shall be confiscated, with the rest of its cargo,—and the owner, purchaser, captain, master, and pilot, shall suffer the punishment of ten years' confinement.

DECREE OF PRESIDENT GUERRERO.
Abolition of Slavery.

The President of the United Mexican States, to the inhabitants of the Republic—

Every apology that has been made in this country for slavery; every argument used in its favor; every instance of apostasy from the ranks of freedom by influential statesmen; every attempt to drag the Bible to the support of the system; and especially every square mile of new territory opened for the introduction of slaves, has contributed to the failure of the efforts to abolish the foreign traffic. The system of slavery, as existing and supported in this

Be it known: That in the year 1829, being desirous of signalizing the anniversary of our independence by an act of national justice and beneficence, which may contribute to the strength and support of such inestimable welfare, as to secure more and more the public tranquillity, and reinstate an unfortunate portion of our inhabitants in the sacred rights granted them by nature, and may be protected by the nation, under wise and just laws, according to the provision in article thirty of the Constitutive act; availing myself of the extraordinary faculties granted me, I have thought proper to decree:

1. That slavery be exterminated in the republic.

2. Consequently those are free, who, up to this day, have been looked upon as slaves.

3. Whenever the circumstances of the public treasury will allow it, the owners of slaves shall be indemnified, in the manner which the laws shall provide.

JOSE MARIA de BOCANEGRA.

Mexico, 15th Sept., 1829, A. D.

[Translation of part of the law of April 6th, 1830, prohibiting the migration of citizens of the United States to Texas.]

ART. 9. On the northern frontier, the entrance of foreigners shall be prohibited, under all pretexts whatever, unless they be furnished with passports, signed by the agents of the republic, at the places whence they proceed.

ART. 10 There shall be no variation with regard to the colonies already established, nor with regard to the slaves that may be in them; but the general government, or the particular state government, *shall take care, under the strictest responsibility, that the colonization laws be obeyed, and that* NO MORE SLAVES BE INTRODUCED.

country, is vitally and indissolubly connected with
the African slave trade. The two are essentially
one. Each inevitably fosters the other. If any great
wickedness is tolerated, it is impossible to control
the shape which that wickedness shall, in all time,
assume. It is natural for it to break out in new
forms, and to grow in strength and power.

The doctrine has been maintained by eminent
divines, that we have nothing to do with slavery in those States where it is an established
institution. Supposing this to be proved, will not
slavery have something to do with us? Can
these teachers of the people and creators of public
opinion imagine for a moment that the master will
lie down in perfect quietness within the limits formerly assigned to him, and have no desire to roam
over new territory? Can his instincts be gratified,
and his fierceness soothed, at the same time?

The extension of slavery and the encouragement
of the slave trade are the natural growth of the
institution of slavery among us. This is abundantly
shown in the annexation of Texas, which is but one
act of several examples that might be adduced.
The determination to secure this country, which
plunged us into a war with Mexico, sprang from a
desire to extend slavery, although at the time, great
efforts were made to blind the eyes of the people to
this fact.

An accurate writer who labored zealously to

enlighten and arouse the public mind on this point, said, in speaking of the war in Texas:

"It is susceptible of the clearest demonstration, that the immediate cause, and the leading object of this contest, originated in a settled design among the slaveholders of this country, (with land speculators and slave traders,) to wrest the large and valuable territory of Texas from the Mexican republic, in order to reëstablish the system of slavery; to open a vast and profitable slave market therein; and, ultimately, to annex it to the United States. And, further, it is evident, — nay, it is very generally acknowledged, — that the insurrectionists are principally citizens of the United States, who have proceeded thither for the purpose of revolutionizing the country; and that they are dependent upon this nation for both the physical and pecuniary means to carry the design into effect. We have a still more important view of the subject. The slaveholding interest is now paramount in the executive branch of our national government; and its influence operates, indirectly, yet powerfully, through that medium, in favor of this grand scheme of oppression and tyrannical usurpation.

    *   *   *   *   *   *

"Such are the motives for action, — such the combination of interests, — such the organization, sources of influence, and foundation of authority, upon which the present Texas insurrection rests. The resident colonists compose but a small fraction of the party concerned in it. The standard of revolt was raised as soon as it was clearly ascertained that slavery could not be perpetuated, nor the illegal speculations in land continued, under the government of the Mexican republic. The Mexican authorities were charged with acts of oppression, while the true causes of the revolt, — the motives and designs of the insurgents, — were studiously concealed from the public view. Influential slaveholders are contributing money, equipping troops, and marching to the scene of conflict. The land speculators are fitting out expeditions from New York and New Orleans, with men, munitions of war, provisions, &c., to promote the object. The independence of Texas is declared, and the system of slavery, as well as the slave trade, (with the United States,) is fully recognized by the government they have set up. Commissioners are sent from the colonies, and agents are appointed here, to make formal application, enlist the sympathies of our citizens, and solicit aid in every way that it can be furnished."

When this iniquity has so far ripened that the national government of the "great republic of liberty" were ready to plunge into a war with Mexico, to reëstablish slavery upon soil from which the curse had been removed, and were searching for pretexts for the war, the Hon. John Quincy Adams, in his speech in the House of Representatives, in May, 1836, said :

" But, sir, it has struck me, as no inconsiderable evidence of the spirit which is spurring us into this war of aggression, of conquest, and of slave-making, that all the fires of ancient, hereditary national hatred are to be kindled, to familiarize us with the ferocious spirit of rejoicing at the massacre of prisoners in cold blood. Sir, is there not yet hatred enough between the races which compose your southern population and the population of Mexico, their next neighbor, but you must go back eight hundred or a thousand years, and to another hemisphere, for the fountains of bitterness between you and them ?   What is the temper of feeling between the component parts of your own southern population, between your Anglo-Saxon, Norman-French, and Moorish-Spanish inhabitants of Louisiana, Mississippi, Arkansas, and Missouri ? between them all and the Indian savage, the original possessor of the land from which you are scourging him already back to the foot of the Rocky Mountains ?   What between them all and the American negro, of African origin, whom they are holding in cruel bondage ?   Are these elements of harmony, concord, and patriotism between the component parts of a nation starting upon a crusade of conquest ?   And what are the feelings of all the motley compound, equally heterogeneous of the Mexican population ?   Do not you, an Anglo-Saxon, slaveholding exterminator of Indians, from the bottom of your soul, hate the Mexican-Spaniard-Indian emancipator of slaves, and abolisher of slavery ?   And do you think that your hatred is not with equal cordiality returned ?   Go to the city of Mexico, — ask any one of your fellow-citizens who have been there for the last three or four years, whether they scarcely dare show their faces, as Anglo-Americans, in the streets.   Be assured, sir, that however heartily you detest the Mexican, his bosom burns with an equally deep-seated detestation of you.

" And this is the nation with which, at the instigation of your executive government, you are now rushing into war, — into a war of conquest, — commenced by aggression on your part, and for the reëstablishment of slavery, where it has been abolished, throughout the Mexican republic.

*   *   *   *   *   *

" And again I ask, what will be your *cause* in such a war? Aggression, conquest, and the reëstablishment of slavery, where it has been abolished.   In that war, sir, the banners of *freedom* will be the banners of Mexico; and your ban-

6

ners, I blush to speak the word, will be the banners of slavery."

The feeling excited in England at the time, by this movement, was very great. The friends of humanity there felt that it would not only embarrass the efforts which were in progress for the suppression of the slave trade, but would actually contribute to the revival of the traffic. And this result we are beginning to experience. The following is taken from the London Times.

"Mr. T. F. Buxton expressed his belief that if the Americans should obtain possession of Texas, which had been truly described as forming one of the fairest harbors in the world, a greater impulse would be given to the slave trade than had been experienced for many years. If the British government did not interfere to prevent the Texan territory from falling into the hands of the American slaveholders, in all probability a greater traffic in slaves would be carried on during the next fifty years, than had ever before existed. The war at present being waged in Texas, differed from any war which had ever been heard of.

"It was not a war for the extension of territory, — it was not a war of aggression, — it was not one undertaken for the advancement of national glory; it was a war which had for its sole object the obtaining of a market for slaves — [Hear, hear.] He would not say that the American government connived at the proceedings which had taken place; but it was notorious that the Texans had been supplied with munitions of war of all sorts, by the slaveholders of the United States — [Hear, hear.] Without meaning to cast any censure upon the government, he thought that the House had a right to demand that the Secretary for Foreign Affairs adopt strong measures to prevent the establishment of a new and more extensive market for the slave trade than had ever before existed."

Before the tribunal of Heaven, before the court of civilization, our nation must stand condemned of the guilt of placing obstacles in the way of the abolition of the slave trade. The nation, of all others, which the world had a right to expect would do her duty upon this question, has been false to the first principles of justice, false to the common dictates of humanity. The great free republic has stretched out her arm to prevent Europe from breaking off the fetters from the enslaved children of Africa. What a chapter in the history of America for the historian to write two centuries hence! But a darker chapter is just now opening. Another harvest from the seeds of iniquity that have been scattered broadcast over the land, is beginning to ripen.

CHAPTER VI.

EVIDENCES OF THE REVIVAL OF THE SLAVE TRADE IN THE UNITED STATES.

Isaiah i. 4. Ah, sinful nation, a people laden with iniquity, a seed of evil-doers, children that are corrupters: they have forsaken the Lord, they have provoked the Holy One of Israel unto anger, they are gone away backward.

St. James v. 1. Go to now, *ye* rich men, weep and howl for your miseries that shall come upon *you*.

4. Behold, the hire of the laborers who have reaped down your fields, which is of you kept back by fraud, crieth: and the cries of them which have reaped are entered into the ears of the Lord of Sabaoth.

5. Ye have lived in pleasure on the earth, and been wanton; ye have nourished your hearts, as in a day of slaughter.

6. Ye have condemned *and* killed the just; *and* he doth not resist you.

Ecclesiastes viii. 11. Because sentence against an evil work is not executed speedily, therefore the heart of the sons of men is fully set in them to do evil.

E'en now, e'en now, on yonder western shores,
Weeps pale Despair, and writhing Anguish roars;
E'en now in Afric's groves, with hideous yell,
Fierce SLAVERY stalks and slips the dogs of hell;
From vale to vale the gathering cries rebound,
And sable nations tremble at the sound.
Who right the injured, and reward the brave,
Stretch your strong arm, for ye have power to save.
Throned in the vaulted heart, his dread resort,
Inexorable CONSCIENCE holds his court;
With still small voice the plots of guilt alarms,
Bares his masked brow, his lifted hand disarms;
But, wrapped in night, with terrors all his own,
He speaks in thunders when the deed is done.
Hear him, ye Senates: hear this truth sublime,
He who allows oppression shares the crime.
                                        ERASMUS DARWIN.

It would be a libel upon the Southern States of our confederacy to say that, as a body, they were in favor of the revival of the slave trade, or to say that the southern people were unanimous in their approval of slavery.

We know, from personal acquaintance, that there are many noble men and women at the South, who see and acknowledge the evils of the system, and deeply deplore its existence. There are thousands, also, who abhor the slave trade, and deprecate the efforts that are being made for its resuscitation. And our desire is to fortify such in their opinions, and secure their coöperation with the power of the North and West, in resisting those efforts. Unless there is such coöperation, to enlighten the people in reference to the dangers that threaten them, the public opinion may become corrupt upon this topic, as it has in years past upon other questions growing out of slavery.

Some may take the ground that the foreign slave trade is an evil too stupendous to allow us to think for a moment of its extensive revival in this country. But does history prove that this country is averse to fostering stupendous evils? Has the government, or the people, shown any great timidity in trampling under foot the principles of right, the dictates of humanity, the pledges of the past? Have solemn contracts preserved soil consecrated to freedom from the invasion of the slave power? Has an enlightened conscience secured deference to God's government, when the laws of human government have clashed with it? Do not multitudes regard the sentiment of a "higher law" as a jest? an "overruling Providence" as an obsolete idea?

The traffic is conducted with so much secrecy, and such vigilance is exercised to escape detection, that it is difficult to obtain full evidence of its extent in this country. Still, there is proof enough to show that it is carried on in Cuba and Brazil to an alarming degree, and that American citizens are guilty of participating in it.

The state of the trade at the present time may be learned from Harper's Cyclopædia of Commerce, published in New York, in 1858, — a reliable authority. Under the article "Slave Trade," * the following statement is made:

"Passing over the interval from the period when the slave trade was declared to be piracy, to the year 1840, we find the number introduced into Brazil from that year to 1851, inclusive, was 348,609, or a little more than 30,000 a year. During the same period, the number imported into Cuba amounted to an average of about 6,000 a year. . . . . As perhaps not more than three fourths of the whole number was reported to the mixed commission, the yearly average for this period, (for both countries,) may be set down at 45,000. . . . . The slave trade is now mainly, if not wholly, carried on with Cuba, which imports about 20,000 slaves every year; which added to the total of the trade with both Brazil and Cuba, since the year 1850, gives the

* Page 1728.

average number imported every year up to the present time, at about 30,000. If the profit realized on the purchase of one slave amounts, as we have shown, to $365, the total profits of one year's trade will therefore be about $11,-000,000.   *   *   *   *

"It is estimated that in the port of New York alone, about twelve vessels are fitted out every year for the slave trade, and that Boston and Baltimore furnish each about the same number, making a fleet of thirty-six vessels, all engaged in a commerce at which the best feelings of our nature revolt. If to these be added the slavers fitted out in other Eastern ports besides Boston, we will have a total of about forty, which is rather under than over the actual number. Each slaver registers from 150 to 250 tons, and costs, when ready for sea, with provisions, slave equipments, and every thing necessary for a successful trip, about $8,000.

"Here, to start with, we have a capital of $320,000, the greater part of which is contributed by Northern men."

A table of costs is then given, and, —

"From this estimate, it will be seen that the amount of capital required to fit out a fleet of slavers, is about $1,500,000, upon which the profits are so immense as almost to surpass belief. In a single voyage of the fleet, 24,000 human beings are carried off from different points on the slave coasts; and of these, 4000, or one sixth of the whole number, become victims to the horrors of the middle passage, leaving 20,000 fit for market. For each of these, the trader obtains an average of $500, making a total for the whole 20,000 of $10,000,000.

"Now if we estimate the number of trips made by each vessel in a year at two, we will have this increased to $20,-000,000. Each vessel, it is true, can make three, and sometimes four trips; but as some are destroyed after the first voyage, we have placed the number at the lowest estimate. The expenses and profits of the slave trade for a single year, compare as follows:

Total expenses of two voyages, - - - $3,000,000
Total receipts of two voyages, - - - 20,000,000

Profits, - - - - $17,000,000 "

The case of the slave yacht Wanderer is fresh in the memories of the people. Her cargo of human beings has been distributed over various plantations, the slaves having been sold for $800 and $1000 each, and some even as high as $1500. Against the captain the Grand Jury for the District of Georgia found indictments, but the United States Judge in South Carolina refused to issue a warrant for his arrest. So much for justice, and obedience to the laws of the land!

The Echo was seized in the act of attempting to land slaves on the coast of Cuba. The bark E. A. Rawlins was seized in the bay of St. Joseph, where she had taken upon herself the new name of Rosa Lee. Last December, she cleared from Savannah, with rice on board. At that time there were suspicions that she was a slaver, but she escaped. Two and a half months later, she was taken in St. Joseph's bay, an unfrequented place, westward of Apalachicola River. There was abundant evidence to believe that she had been to Africa, taken on board her living freight, subjected the victims to all the horrors of the "middle passage," and landed them at Cuba and on the coast of the Gulf of Mexico.

A suspicious looking vessel was seen off the mouth of the Apalachicola, avoiding the pilots who approached her, her papers irregular, and the captain having taken an assumed name. A Spanish captain had been on board, who, the crew confessed, had been murdered.

Another case occurred near Mobile, and the crew were arrested, and brought before the Grand Jury of South Carolina. But these grave representatives of American justice, these protectors of innocence, refused to find indictments against the guilty men, and the United States judge for that district was equally resolute in refusing to enforce the laws against the slave trade.

So bold are some in their movements, that recently imported Africans are publicly offered for sale. The following is from the Richmond Reporter, (Texas,) of the 14th of June, 1859:

FOR SALE. — Four hundred likely African negroes, lately landed upon the coast of Texas. Said negroes will be sold upon the most reasonable terms. One third down ; the remainder in one or two years, with eight per cent. interest. For further information, inquire of C. K. C., Houston, or L. R. G., Galveston.

And the Tribune quotes from the Vicksburg True Southron of the 13th, an account of an African Labor Supply Association, of which the Hon. J. B. D. De Bow is President.

Thus it is evident that this trade is to be encouraged in defiance of law, and organized efforts are to be made to secure the repeal of the laws enacted by our fathers against this evil.

A Washington correspondent of the New York Herald, said to be an accurate and reliable writer, stated, on the authority of a United States senator, that the number of cargoes of African slaves landed on the coast of the United States, and smuggled into the interior, since May, 1858, a period of fifteen months, amounts to sixty or seventy,* and twelve vessels more are expected within ninety days. If grand juries and judges refuse to enforce the laws against the slave trade, it may be indefinitely increased. And from despatches received at the Navy Department, from the frigate Cumberland, dated at Porto Praya, April 15, 1859, it appears that during the last year the traffic has greatly increased. Those despatches state that yachts, schooners, and trading vessels are engaged in the business, and that small armed vessels are required, that can sail up the rivers and capture the slavers.

To encourage the trade, it is stated that eighteen slaveholders in Enterprise, Miss., recently pledged themselves to buy 1000 negroes, at a certain price, if they were brought from Africa.

But I will let the southern papers and politicians speak for themselves. They have spoken, and their dark schemes of infamy and cruelty are before the nation.

* This is higher than the estimate in Harper's Cyclopædia, but that writer thinks that he understates the actual number.

The Apalachicola (Fla.) Advertiser says:

"Until the slave trade is opened and made legal, the South will push slavery forward, as a seasoning for every dish. This is the settled and determined policy of a party at the South. We do not pretend to belong to the ultra-southern party, but we believe it a duty which the general government owes to the South, that the slave trade should be legitimate, that her vast domain may receive cultivation."

If this paper does not belong to the ultra southern party, we should be glad to have it define its position. If there is any wickedness, beyond rendering "the slave trade legitimate," we have yet to be informed of it.

In April, 1859, the citizens of Metagorda, Texas, passed the following resolution:

"*Resolved*, That our delegates to the Convention be requested to inquire into the expediency of obtaining negro laborers suited to our climate and products, from some foreign country, and recommend measures by which the importation can be carried on under the supervision and protection of the State."

At a meeting held in Hanesville, Appling County, Georgia, Col. Goulding, of Liberty, (!) offered several resolutions, which were adopted, one of which was, "that all laws of the federal government, interdicting the right of the southern people to import slaves from Africa, are unconstitutional, and violative of the rights of the South; and that said laws are null and void, and a disgrace to the statute book."

The New York Tribune of March 17, 1859, states that Dr. Daniel Lee, Professor of Agriculture and kindred sciences in the Georgia University, has written a letter in favor of reopening the slave trade, — or, rather, in favor of African importations, — the better to develop the agricultural resources of the South.

The necessity of more slaves to develop the resources of the South, and settle new territories, is becoming a favorite argument with the advocates of the revival of the foreign trade. And it will doubtless become more and more prominent in the discussions which the subject of the African trade will awaken in the future.

The Augusta Constitutionalist reports the speech delivered by the Hon. A. H. Stephens to a large concourse of people assembled in the City Park Hall, in July last, on the occasion of his resignation as representative in Congress, when he used the following language:

" As he said, in 1850, he would repeat now, there is very little prospect of the South settling any territory outside of Texas; in fact, little or no prospect at all, unless we increase our African stock.

" The question his hearers should examine in its length and breadth ; he would do nothing more than present it ; but it is as plain as any thing, that unless the number of African stock be increased, we have not the population, and might as well abandon the race with our brethren cf the North, *in the colonization of the territories.* It was not for him to

advise on these questions: he only presented them. The
people should think and act upon them. If there are but
few more slave States, it is not because of abolitionism, or the
Wilmot Proviso, but simply for the want of people to settle
them. We can not make States without people; rivers and
mountains do not make them; and slave States *can not be
made without Africans.*"

This language was addressed to the gentlemen
and ladies of the city, and is˜said to have been received with great applause.

At Fort Valley, Ga., there is published a newspa-
per, called "The Nineteenth Century," which holds
the following language in regard to the slave trade:

"Necessity will demand it at no distant day, and we also
believe that the necessity will bring about the object of itself, without much noise or confusion on the part of the
southern people."

So it seems that the flood gates of this stream of
moral and physical death are to be opened quietly,
without much disturbance of the public conscience,
a few slight tremors, perhaps, and without much
"noise" from that unfortunate class whose nerves
are affected by the horrors of the middle passage.
Perhaps the soothing influences of the "Nineteenth
Century" will aid in this matter, and the introduction of modern improvements may render the African more submissive to his fate.

There is still another argument for the revival of

the slave trade alluded to by the "Southern Confederacy," published at Atlanta, Ga.

That paper declares, that "The African slave trade is the hope and bulwark of southern interests. It is the basis underlying the future greatness and permanency of the slave States. Without its establishment, the institution (slavery) will soon become useless."

We have said that there was a vital connection between American slavery and the African slave trade, and here we have one of the proofs. We see the direct result of the doctrine which has been so strenuously maintained, that the institution should not be meddled with where it was established. As well might we be told, You must not touch the roots of the tree, but if the branches should spread too widely, or the fruits become too bitter, these points may be carefully and judiciously considered! The principle laid down in Matthew iii. 10, is: "And now also the axe is laid unto the root of the trees; therefore every tree which bringeth not forth good fruit is hewn down and cast into the fire."

The word "piracy" greatly troubles the friends of the slave trade. In May, 1859, at a meeting held in Parker County, Texas, it was

"*Resolved*, That we demur to any law of Congress making the foreign slave trade piracy, as a usurpation of power not warranted by the Constitution of the United States, and ought to be repealed."

We come now to a document that deserves our careful attention. In May, the Savannah Republican published an indignant protest of the grand jury which recently indicted parties suspected of being engaged in the slave trade. The jurymen, being under oath to find a bill according to law, state that they did so *against their will.* The protest concludes thus:

" Heretofore, the people of the South, firm in their consciousness of right and strength, have failed to place the stamp of condemnation upon such laws as reflect upon the institution of slavery, but have permitted, unrebuked, the influence of foreign opinion to prevail in their support.

" Longer to yield to a sickly sentiment of pretended philanthropy, and diseased mental observation of ' higher law ' fanatics, the tendency of which is to debase us in the estimation of civilized nations, is weak and unwise. They then unhesitatingly advocate the repeal of all laws which directly or indirectly condemn the institution, and think it the duty of the southern people to require their legislators to unite their efforts for the accomplishment of this object." (Signed)

CHARLES GRANT,	BENEDICT BOURGEIN,
H. S. BYRD, M. D.,	JNO. J. JACKSON,
S. PALMER,	GEO. W. GARMY.

This is certainly a very remarkable production. That it represents an extensive southern opinion, we will not believe without farther evidence. Its authors are alone responsible for it.

We know that such sentiments are received with disgust by thousands at the South. Many distin-

guished men have already spoken out against the
slave trade. Let such men be multiplied and sustained, and the South may be saved from self-
destruction, and the nation from the guilt of that
gigantic crime into which many are so madly
plunging.

We rejoice that our northern State legislatures
are waking up to the magnitude of this evil.

The following resolution against this traffic was
passed April 12, 1859, by the New York State Assembly, by a vote of 101 to 6:

"*Resolved*, (if the Senate concur,) That the citizens of
this State look with surprise and detestation upon the vir-
tual opening of the slave trade within the Federal Union :
that against this invasion of our laws, of our feelings, and of
the dictates of Christianity, we solemnly protest : that we call
upon the citizens of the Union to make cause in the name
of religion and humanity, and as friends of the principles
underlying our system of government, to unite in bringing
to immediate arrest and punishment all persons engaged in
the unlawful and wicked trade, and hereby instruct our sen-
ators and representatives in Congress to exert all lawful
power for the immediate suppression of this infamous traffic.

"*Resolved*, That the Executive of this State be required
to transmit a copy of this resolution to the legislatures of the
several States of this Union, and earnestly request their
coöperation in arresting this great wickedness."

Would that every legislature that professes to
love liberty, would follow the noble example set by
the Empire State! Would that every representa-

tive would recall to his memory the words of the
gifted and eloquent Webster, as uttered in his speech
on the President's protest:

"We have been taught to regard a representative of the
people as a sentinel upon the watch-tower of liberty. Is he
to be blind, though visible danger approaches ? Is he to be
deaf, though sounds of peril fill the air ? Is he to be dumb,
while a thousand duties impel him to raise the cry of alarm ?
Is he not rather to catch the lowest whisper that breathes intention or purpose of encroachment on the public liberties,
and to give his voice, breath, and utterance at the first ap-
pearance of danger ? Is not his eye to traverse the whole
horizon, with the keen and eagle vision of an unhooded
hawk, detecting through all disguises, every enemy, ad-
vancing in any form towards the citadel he guards ? "

7

CHAPTER VII.

CONCLUSION.

Isa. lviii. 1. "Cry aloud, spare not: lift up thy voice like a trumpet, and shew my people their transgression, and the house of Jacob their sin."

WE have considered in the preceding chapters the cruelties and horrors of the slave trade; the desolating influence of the traffic upon Africa; the efforts made to abolish the evil; and the evidence of its continuance, and of the attempts to revive the trade.

It only remains for us to allude to some of the inevitable effects of reopening a traffic, so revolting to every feeling of humanity, every dictate of conscience, and every law of God.

There is no need of extended argument to show that the importation of Africans into this country would directly and fearfully augment that evil which already to so great an extent is paralyzing industry, blighting commerce, and destroying the best interests of society. The disastrous influence of American slavery upon agriculture, the mechanical arts, education, public virtue, religion, has been fully set forth by others. Measures have been proposed to mitigate the evils growing out of the system, and good men, North and South, have looked forward to the time when the nation would be relieved of this burden. But the revival of the foreign traffic will perpetuate and extend the system, and blast the hopes that have been entertained of its speedy removal. It will embarrass every measure for the elevation and improvement of those in bondage, tighten the chains of the oppressed, and discourage all effort at even gradual emancipation.

The establishment of the American slave trade would also be a source of irritation between the North and South. Already the ill feeling produced by the encroachments of slavery is sundering fraternal relations, impeding the progress of trade, and exasperating one portion of the community against another. And let this additional firebrand be thrown in, and the flames of animosity would be kindled over the whole country.

On the one side would be this evil, with its cruelties, its violation of all the principles of justice and humanity ; and on the other the intelligence, moral rectitude, and Christian virtue of millions of freemen. And to suppose that these elements can lie quietly side by side, is to suppose an utter impossibility. Our system of education must be corrupted to the very core ; our literature must be poisoned by the sentiments of the dark ages ; all traces of right and justice must be obliterated from our statute books, and our religion must become a dead form, before such a result can be anticipated. Oil and water will not mingle. Barbarism and Christianity were not made to dwell together in peace.

We should also consider the inevitable effect of this evil upon the pulpits and churches of our land. Ministers of the gospel must either preach against this sin, or be corrupted and weakened by it. Professing Christians must oppose it, or yield to it. And what must be the character of a church for purity, efficiency, and spiritual power, that tolerates such an iniquity? What would be its influence in converting men to the principles of brotherly love, self-denial, faith, and holiness taught by our Saviour? Is it to be supposed that impenitent men will close their eyes to such gross inconsistencies?

Every man's common sense teaches him that the power of the gospel lies in its purity, and in its hostility to every form of sin. The instant it compromises with evil, it ceases to be the gospel of Jesus Christ.

In conclusion, it is the solemn duty of every American patriot and Christian to rise up and decree that, let the consequences be what they may, another slave shall never pollute our coast, and that, God helping them, they will resist now and for ever, every attempt to revive this accursed traffic. To allow it, is to increase and perpetuate the evils that to-day threaten the very existence of the republic. It puts in peril the American Union, and what is more, endangers the liberties of the whole nation. No greater calamity could befall us, no greater curse could smite us, than the reopening of the slave trade. War, pestilence, and famine might not damage us as much as this iniquity. For we might resist the war, and recover from the effects of the pestilence and famine, but this accursed thing strikes at the vitals of the republic. It breaks down the principles of the nation. It corrupts the morals, poisons the religion, and exposes us to the burning wrath of Jehovah.

Should we in this enlightened age sanction such a wickedness, we should deserve to perish. If the heroes of the American revolution saw the inconsistency of appealing to the God of freedom to aid them in their struggle, and then turning round to put chains upon their fellow men, how much more glaring the inconsistency and stupendous the wickedness for us, while in the enjoyment of all the blessings of freedom, to use our power to enslave others, and deprive them of privileges that we would die rather than part with ourselves. And the meanness of such a course is as great as its guilt.

We appeal to the patriotism of American citizens, and we ask them whether they are willing to see this great republic, freighted with so many human hopes, blessed as it has been of heaven, sacrificed at the altar of this great iniquity? Shall we peril the brilliant prospects of the nation, provoke the wrath of God, become a hissing and a by-word throughout Christendom, by madly clinging to that which is evil, and only evil, and that continually?

I know of no spectacle so full of cheering hope and moral sublimity, as to see this nation, to-day, rise up in her strength and declare that the slaver shall not touch our coast, that the virgin soil of the country shall not be polluted by the invasion of slavery, and that we will as speedily as possible throw off this burden from the ship of state, in order that, with every sail spread and the banner of freedom nailed to the mast-head, we may ride on triumphantly, fulfilling our great mission among the nations of the earth.

In this work there rests upon the church of Christ a vast responsibility. Every individual member is responsible for his opinion, his influence, and his action. And I believe that the American church has the power to decide this question. The slave trade and slavery can not stand against the united force of the pulpits and churches of the country. The triumph of Christianity will be the destruction of slavery.

www.ingramcontent.com/pod-product-compliance
Lightning Source LLC
Chambersburg PA
CBHW030837300326
41935CB00037B/591